To Mother & Father

Love & Best Wishes

Christmas 1977.

Holly David Suzanne & Jeremy.

x x x

# A Victorian Village

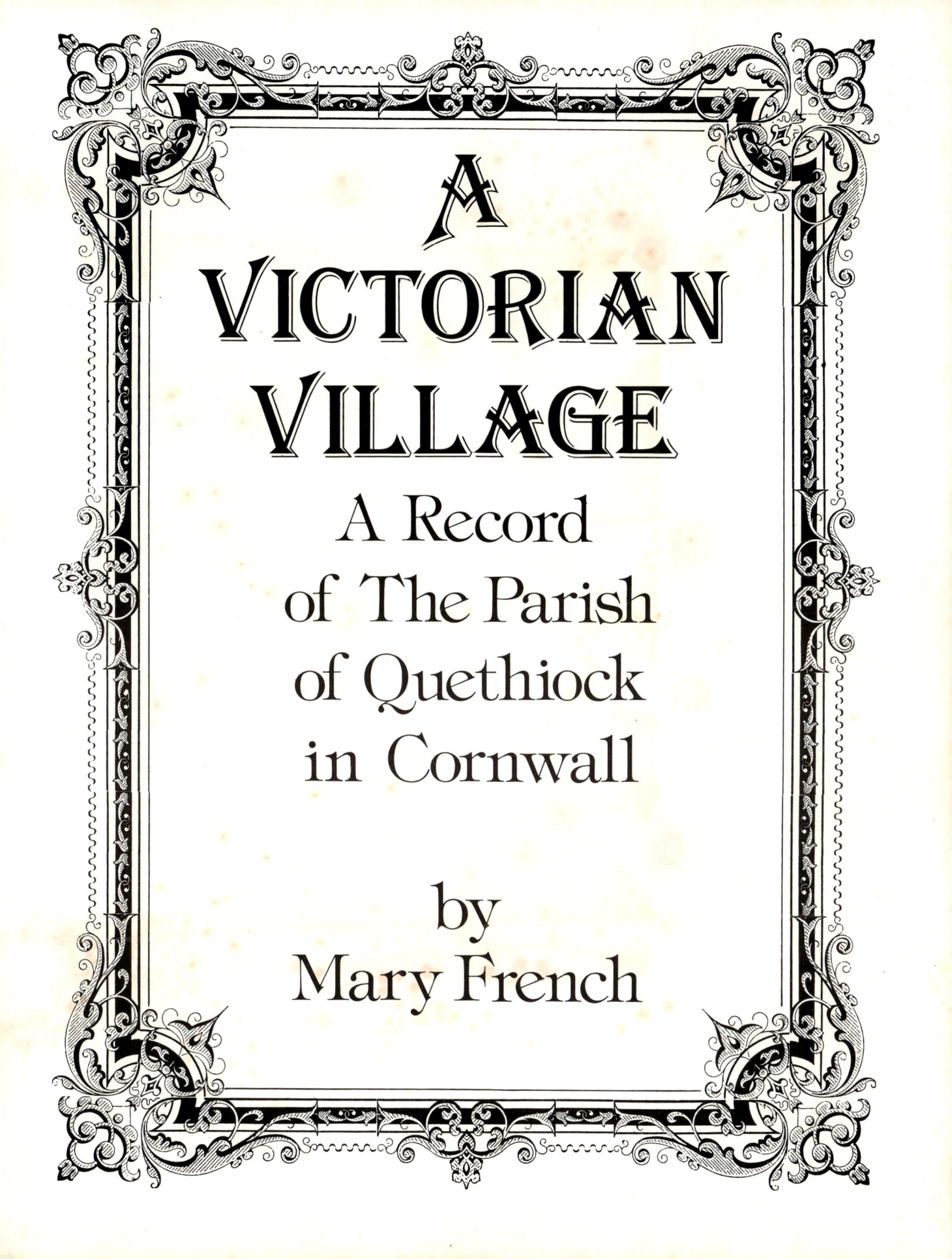

A Record of The Parish of Quethiock in Cornwall

by

Mary French

VENNING'S NEW CENTURY MAP OF EAST CORNWALL. 1901.

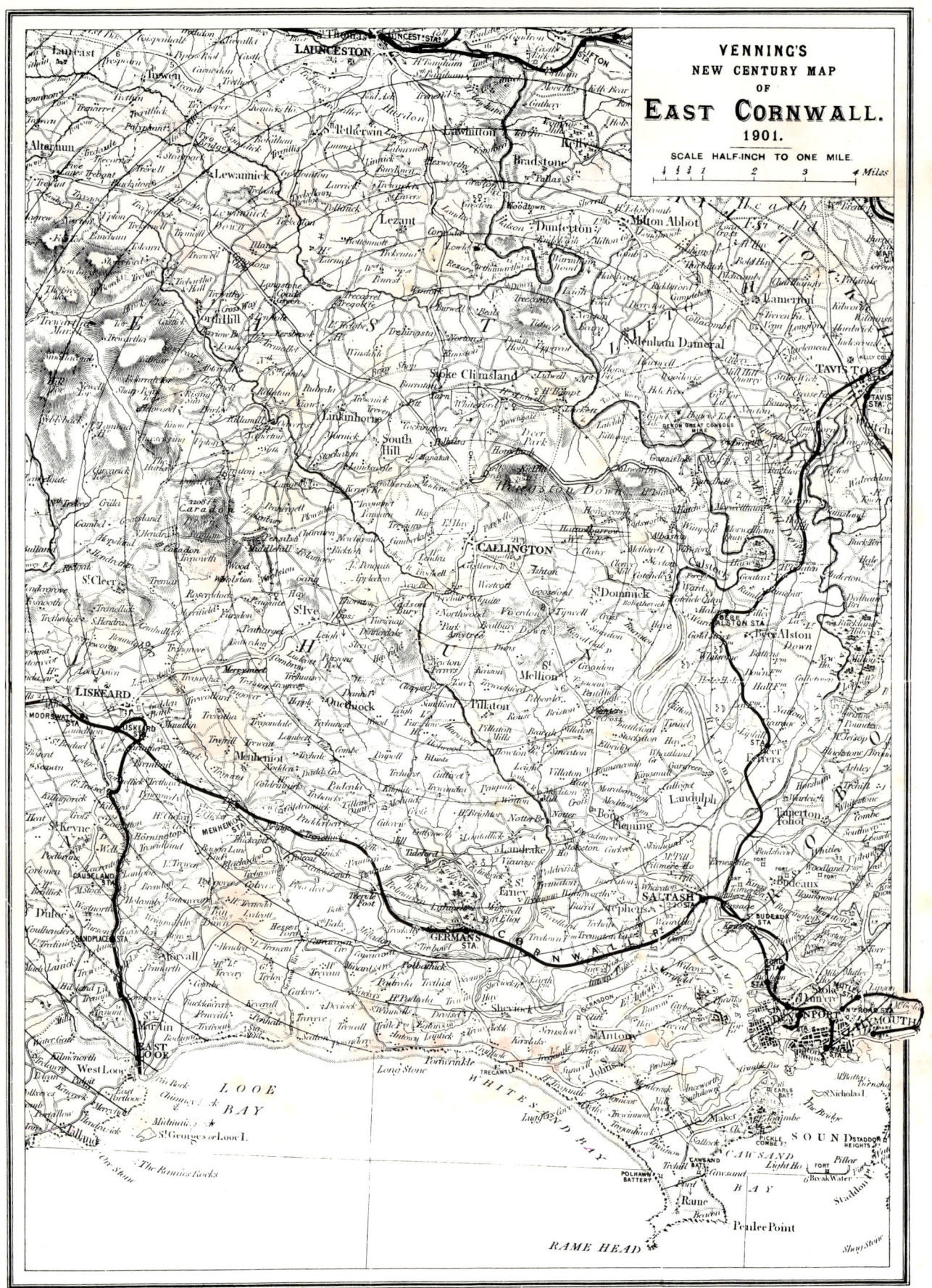

SCALE HALF-INCH TO ONE MILE

Published and sold by J. Venning, Post Office, Callington.

**THE DISTANCE BETWEEN EACH CIRCLE IS ONE MILE.**

Gall & Inglis, Edinburgh.

# CONTENTS

| | |
|---|---|
| Foreword | 6 |
| The Sale of Quethiock | 6.8.10.12.14.15 |
| The Squires | 17.18.20.21.23.26.27.29.30.32.33 |
| The Larger Farms | 35.36.38.39.41.42.43.45.46.47.49.50.51 |
| The Smaller Farms | 56.57.58.60.61.63.64.66.67 |
| The School | 70.72.74.75.78 |
| The Leisure | 81.83.85.87.89 |
| The Chapels | 91.93.94.96.97.99.100 |
| The Church | 102.104.105.106.109.110 |
| Acknowledgements | 112 |

Published by

# GLASNEY PRESS

Falmouth

*Quethiock village, looking west, with the Parish Church of St. Hugh's, the Celtic Cross and Well Cottages. Late 19th century.*

*The main street of the village in 1900. Mr Heddon's famous fruit garden is on the left, then the shop, newly built in 1898, by Squire William Coryton, for the growing family of Mr Alfred Harris. The National School is the last building in the row.*

## FOREWORD

*The subject of this study is the parish of Quethiock, pronounced 'Quithik', in Cornwall, Great Britain, around the turn of the 19th century. It may seem, at first glance, to be one of purely local interest, parochial in the narrow sense of the word, that is, of little general importance. It is a record in words and photographs of a thriving and happy rural community which had survived intact from medieval days, having kept for all this time the same family of Squires, the same tribes of tenant farmers, and the same systems of land tenure and husbandry. Its people had therefore entirely escaped the bitterness and demoralisation that followed the English Enclosures and the Scottish Clearances. Nevertheless, when after 1919 this fortunate little community began to disintegrate because of the sale of the parish it was of no concern elsewhere, not a ripple of doubt stirred the complacency of an industrialised nation. What mattered if one more close-knit community be scattered?*

*Today we are beginning to know better. We are beginning to understand that the destruction of any rural community, however apparently insignificant, is ultimately of global concern. Some of the consequences are already painfully plain to see, particularly in the miles of shameful shanty-towns that ring so many of the world's fine cities. Here, in squalid 'barriadas' and 'bustees', in dark caves in hillsides, even sharing tombs with the dead, dwell millions of ex-country folk who have lost not only hope and dignity but also the capacity to feed themselves. For them, as for half the world's total population, malnutrition and even famine are ever-present menaces. As this hungry half of the world grows in numbers so does the threat to world peace. It is a greater threat, possibly, even than that posed by our annual spending of an astronomical £80,000 million on arms, which includes some £8,000 million on preparations for nuclear war, altogether about one-tenth of total world income.*

*Whether the rich and powerful nations of our crazy world can change their priorities in time to avoid catastrophe will be seen within the next fifty years, roughly the same span of time that has elapsed since the great world exodus to the cities began. At present there is little sign of it. The developed nations are not yet practising what their most advanced thinkers are preaching, namely following a policy of reasonable self-sufficiency in food production, and of a careful and comprehensive conservation of resources, of keeping small communities on the land, and of all, those in cities and villages alike, being encouraged to live simply, to work hard and to waste nothing. Certainly there will be no shortage of specialists – economists, industrialists, politicians and the like – to foregather in expensively convened conferences in order to discuss the problems of the conflicting interests of city versus countryside, nor will there be any shortage of intellectuals from university and government-financed research institutes to debate, at equally expensive length, the complex issues involved. They will have one thing in common, that they depend on the labour of others for their daily bread. There is already in existence an International Institute for Applied Systems Analysis, housed in a magnificent castle near Vienna, where eminent scientists from many countries are developing and applying methods of systems analysis, management theory and computer science to the complex and interdisciplinary problems occurring in modern societies. It is unlikely that many working farmers or their wives will be invited to these gatherings. Perhaps it would have brought urgency to the discussions were they held, not in a fine castle, but in the centre of a shanty-town, desperately lacking in piped water and proper sewage facilities! AND IN FOOD!*

*Here, by way of contrast, is a study by a working farmer's wife of a small Cornish community that had few of the rural problems now causing global concern. Today one of the chief shadows over the future is the question of what will happen when oil runs out. We evade the issue because we are afraid to face it. In the developed countries farming now depends absolutely upon oil, not only for operating the many machines which have replaced men and horses, but also to manufacture the chemical fertilisers, the pesticides and herbicides that modern methods of farming have made necessary.*

*Quethiock, at the time I shall describe, still had its men and horses. It used a little paraffin in its lamps. It had no tractors. It had no need to worry about the price of food for it grew most of what it ate, nor about the cost of electricity for it had none, nor of coal for its burned its own wood. It was an astonishingly self-reliant parish, a community whose values were quite different from ours today. Those values had strength. Our frenzied squandering of the earth's precious resources is already doomed as a way of life. The story that follows may perhaps help to illuminate our way back to that simpler life which is inevitable if we are to survive peacefully and happily into the twenty-first century.*

# The Sale of the Parish of Quethiock

The date was August 14th, 1919, the place a public room in the Royal Hotel, Plymouth. Britain's National Peace Day had only recently been celebrated. The ending of the years of tremendous effort and of terrible sacrifice — some twenty million soldiers and civilians dead, twenty million more wounded, another twenty million lost from starvation or from war-spread diseases — the ending of all this had been thankfully and officially celebrated on July 19th, with dancing crowds, with flags, banners, festoons, illuminations and fireworks. Enthusiastic Peace Celebration Committees had organised all manner of feasts and festivities. The warriors were coming home at last, coming home to peace, to a grateful country that could now return to normal life. Or so almost everyone believed. Who could then foresee that the drastic, punitive terms of the Armistice that ended the First World War had already sown the bitter seeds of the Second, and had already ensured that never again would there be any return to 'normal' in the old, comfortable pre-war sense?

Meanwhile there were many immediate problems to be solved. Ration Books, first issued in July, 1918, were due to be renewed, for sugar, meat and fats were still in very short supply. Work, too, must be found for the returning ex-servicemen. How better thought the Government, in a rare mood of inspiration, than to kill two birds with one stone by encouraging some of these men to settle on the land. To this end it proposed to finance the buying of farms for them, farms large enough to be capable of division into smallholdings which could then be rented. Thus many deserving men could be given useful, healthy work and at the same time the nation would be provided with more food. It was an excellent scheme, on paper. In practice it was to bring many problems. Especially to Quethiock.

Although peace had been declared nationally, the scene in the crowded hotel room in Plymouth on that August afternoon in 1919 was very far from peaceful. No doubt to the anxious auctioneer, who soon began to watch passions running dangerously high, it must have appeared as though a riot were imminent. The large crowd, mostly of farmers, had been gathered together by an advertisement which had now been appearing for some weeks in various local newspapers, as, for example, on the front page of *The Cornish Times* for July 18th 1919.

**East Cornwall**

Highly Important Sale of a Valuable Freehold Estate of about 4,200 acres.
Whitton & Laing are favoured with instructions to
SELL BY AUCTION (in numerous lots)
at The Royal Hotel, Plymouth
on Thursday, the 14th day of August 1919, at 2 p.m. precisely,
the very valuable Freehold Property known as
THE QUETHIOCK ESTATE
situated in the Parishes of Quethiock and St Ive and comprising the following
Corn, Sheep and Dairy Farms
with Woods and Plantations and Valuable Sporting Rights.

| | | | |
|---|---|---|---|
| Holwood Farm | about 456 acres | Trebrown Farm | about 167 acres |
| Trehunsey Farm | about 300 acres | West Trehunist Farm | about 166 acres |
| Leigh Farm | about 242 acres | Trenance Farm | about 153 acres |
| Furslow Farm | about 225 acres | Dannett Farm | about 147 acres |
| Trecorme Farm | about 193 acres | East Quethiock | about 144 acres |
| Hammett Farm | about 175 acres | Treweese Farm | about 135 acres |
| Haye Farm | about 172 acres | Hepwell Farm | about 129 acres |
| Goodmerry Farm | about 170 acres | | |

*Miss Ann Rickard, who died in 1909, aged 100, is sitting in a chair outside the Quethiock Almhouses, built and endowed by Walter Coryton in 1633 for 4 spinsters. Later spinsters became scarce, so in 1967 the Almhouses were sold and a Trust Fund created. By 1973, despite the Trustees desperate pleading, not one poor parish spinster could be found.*

*The main street of Blunts, about two miles from Quethiock, with various members of the Jane family in the picture, including 7 children. Mr and Mrs James Jane reared 9 children in one of the cottages on the right. The photograph was taken by the Rev. Wix in 1900 and his wife is in the jingle.*

| | | | |
|---|---|---|---|
| Tilland Farm | about 119 acres | Great West Quiethiock Farm | about 67 acres |
| Luccombe Farm | about 109 acres | Great Ley Farm St Ive | about 52 acres |
| E. Trehunist Farm | about 108 acres | Moordown Tenement part St Ive | about 48 acres |
| Penpoll Farm | about 105 acres | Venn Hill Farm | about 43 acres |
| Venn Farm | about 96 acres | Singmoor Farm | about 41 acres |
| Tilland Mill Farm | about 87 acres | Trehurst Farm | about 40 acres |
| Coombe Farm | about 82 acres | Gooseford Farm | about 37 acres |

Also numerous Smallholdings, Accommodation Lands, Mill Properties, "The Mason's Arms" Public House, Quethiock Post & Telegraph Office, Blacksmith's, Wheelwright's and Carpenter's Shops, Quethiock School House, and various Shops Cottages and Gardens, the whole extending to about

4,200 ACRES

and producing an Actual and Estimated Rental of over

£5,500 per annum

Tenants who desire to purchase the holding which they occupy and who wish to leave a proportion of the purchase money left on Mortgage for a period not exceeding five years, should apply direct to the undermentioned Solicitors who are acting for, and will submit any applications received to, the Trustees, Messrs. Rooker, Matthews & Co., Plymouth. Plans, Particulars, Conditions of Sale, together with Orders to View from the Auctioneers, or from Mr. G. Castle, Pentillie Estate Office, St. Mellion, East Cornwall, or from Messrs. Rooker, Matthews & Co. Solicitors, Frankfort Chambers, Plymouth."

So precisely at 2.0 p.m. on the appointed day the sale of the parish of Quethiock had commenced. The Squire, William Coryton of Pentillie Castle, Lord of the Manor of Quethiock and owner of all the farms in the parish except one, lay on his deathbed. Now his tenants had gathered together, as they had done so often in the past at The Mason's Arms in Quethiock village, in order to pay their rents at Ladyday and Michaelmas. But today, in Plymouth, there was no cheerful chatter, no joking or laughter. Many of them realised that there were bound to be changes. Today crucial decisions must be made and the atmosphere in the hot, crowded room was tense. Many of the farmers were hoping to buy their farms, the innkeeper his inn, the village shopkeeper and the craftsmen their premises. Even a number of the cottagers had brought along their savings, hoping to buy the cottages in which they had been born. Neighbours from other parishes were also present, some merely to watch, others hoping to purchase a coveted holding.

Ominously, there were also a few unfamiliar faces, the pale faces of indoor men, official-looking fellows. Although few of the farmers suspected it, officials indeed they were, men sent by the Cornwall County Council to buy farms capable of sub-division under the Land Settlement (Facilities) Act of 1919. As this Act provided that the Ministry of Agriculture would bear the cost, and also the whole of any loss incurred in the operation for a period of six years from March 31st, 1920, the County Council's men could afford to bid generously. The anxious tenants of the Quethiock farms were thus confronted by officials backed by Ministry money and they very soon began to realise that the bidding at this Sale would not be of the neighbourly Cornish traditional kind, by which no man would deliberately over-bid a sitting tenant, provided that the latter could raise a reasonable buying price. No, this was to be a cut-throat affair, a battle without mercy, tenants versus the Cornwall County Council.

*Trecorme Barton farmstead in 1900 when being farmed by Mrs Kelly, widow of Henry Kelly, assisted by her 4 sons and 2 daughters. Behind the barn can be seen a large well-made rick and 11 children were successfully reared in the cottage on the hill.*

*Mr Body, the miller at Trecorme Mill, coming up Mill Hill in his cart to deliver corn. A cow peacefully grazes the hedge with two leisurely attendants. This photograph appeared in the Parish Magazine for October 1900.*

Lot 1 was Trenance Farm, occupied by a member of the Vosper family. The Vospers also farmed Haye and had been doing so for generations. Nevertheless Trenance, "The Exceedingly Valuable and Attractive Dairy and Corn Farm of 153 acres, together with two cottages at Blunts", was very quickly sold, not to the tenant as expected, but to an unknown Mr. Wilson for £6,000, an unheard of price to the unhappy farmers. "Who is this man?" they began asking one another. Lot 2, Luccombe Farm, was tenanted by a member of another family who had also been farming in the parish for generations, one of the Cannons of Hammett. No matter, Luccombe too was knocked down, for £3,300, to this mysterious Mr. Wilson. The same man yet again? Then the news began to race around the room like wildfire. This man was acting as buyer for the Cornwall County Council and he could afford to bid high. So Mr. Wilson went on to buy Tilland Farm, then Trebrown, East Quethiock, Hepwell, Venn, and East and West Trehunist, against a rising tide of furious mutterings from dispossessed farmers. One of them, a bitterly disappointed member of the Kelly clan, from Trehunist, shouted angrily, to Mr. Wilson, "You'm biddin' with tax-payers' money. We'm biddin' with our own". He too had lost his farm. Several men jumped to their feet with furious cries of, "Chuck the b—s out! Chuck the b—s out!", ready for instant action. It must have been a frightening moment for the unfortunate auctioneer but he kept his head. Somehow he managed to calm the angry men and stop a riot, by pointing out that where the County Council had determined to buy a farm it was almost certain to succeed with the aid of its bottomless public purse, so that violent protest was useless.

By the end of the sale only nine of Quethiock's twenty-eight tenant farmers had succeeded in buying their farms. Nine of the largest and best farms had been bought by the County Council, while ten others had changed hands, mostly to farmers from other neighbouring parishes. *The Cornish Times* next day reported that the farm properties had fetched very high prices, adding:— "There was some heart-burning in cases where tenants desired to buy their farms but were outbid by the County's representative. Once or twice when this happened there were pronounced manifestations of displeasure." A euphemism if ever there was one! Of the nine tenants who managed to buy their farms three were Wenmoths, one of them being my husband's grandfather, Joseph Wenmoth of Goodmerry. But one who lost his was my father-in-law, Richard Wenmoth, then only newly established on his own farm and with a young family. He was outbid for Hepwell Farm by the County Council and joined the ranks of all those who in twelve months must find a farm elsewhere. After anxious search he bought Penadlake Farm in Lanreath parish, five miles from Looe and some fourteen miles from Quethiock. So when my husband, James Snell Wenmoth, was four years old the family moved to this new farm and learned to live among strangers.

Poor young Richard Wenmoth must have returned home feeling very despondent on that August evening for not only must he bear the tragic news that he had lost his farm, and his home, to the County Council, but that his wife's brother, then farming Venn, which was her birthplace, had lost his in the same way; moreover that the ranks of relatives, close friends and long-standing neighbours had been sadly thinned.

One can imagine the crowd of bowler-hatted farmers silently dispersing to go their separate ways, most of them heading for the Great Western station at North Road, there to catch the next slow 'down' train. At Saltash, St. German's or Menheniot their traps would be waiting for them in the station yards. They had plenty to think about as they drove home along the familiar lanes, no doubt rehearsing what they would say to those anxiously awaiting the sound of their approach.

What kind of parish was this to be so coveted by the Cornwall County Council? First and foremost it had first-class soil, the kind of sandy loam, rich brown in colour, that will grow a wide variety of crops. Geologically the parish is situated in the calcareous series, chiefly composed of Upper Devonian slates with isolated fingers of spillitic lavas (volcanic rock) curving across it. The soil therefore contrasts sharply with

*A gipsy cart selling 'flaskets' – washing – day clothes baskets – and wicker furniture. The photograph was taken by the Rev. Wix in 1900, outside 'The Butcher's Arms' at St. Ive.*

*Bill Snell, son of Francis Snell of 'The Mason's Arms', who preferred farming and gave up the licence in 1922. He is here seen with his cart in Quethiock's "busy" main street.*

that covering the granite of Bodmin Moor, to the north, and of the culm in St. Mellion, to the east. The enclosure and subsequent first ploughing of Viverdon Down, in St. Mellion, undertaken from 1893 onward by Squire William Coryton and his Bailiff, John Petherick, was a tremendous task made infinitely harder by the typical poor drainage and the sharp flinty stones of the culm measures. By contrast with these parishes on granite and on culm, Quethiock was an extremely fertile area with easy-working soil, totalling some 4,562 acres, including rivers, roads and wastes.

It is situated some fourteen miles east of Plymouth via the Tamar crossing which was until recent years by Ferry, and lies between two main roads that run westward from the Devon border to Liskeard, and onward to Truro. From either road it can only be approached through narrow, winding lanes. In Victorian days Quethiock must have seemed to live in a small secret world of its own, lost to the greater one except when visited by the Hunt or other sportsmen, or once a year by the crowds that thronged to Quethiock Fair. The parish is longer than it is wide, basically sloping gently from north to south, from the 500' contour at its boundary with St. Ive, not far from Bodmin Moor, to its southern tip not far from tide level. The River Lynher, a clear salmon and trout river, forms the eastern boundary and the River Tiddy the western one. They are fast-flowing rivers, so too is Hay Lake, another smaller stream that bisects the parish before joining the Tiddy. Quethiock has therefore always had abundant water-power of which it made full use until recent times. The majority of the larger farms drove their threshing machines and barn machinery by water-wheels. Trecorme Mill was the principal parish Mill with its own miller in 1919, but as late as 1910 other mills were working. Rainfall was also ample, in fact sometimes too ample according to the following verse:—

### Quethiock Weather

The south wind always brings wet weather;
The north wind, wet and cold together.
The west wind always brings us rain,
The east wind blows it back again.

A contour map of the parish shows an area of great complexity, almost as though some demented giant had left thumbprints all over a piece of parchment. This is a parish of gently rolling hills and sheltered leafy valleys, a place of many strongly rising springs that give birth to sturdy streamlets. It is a fascinatingly varied country that compels the infrequent walker through its high-hedged lanes to pause and lean over every field-gate in order to enjoy ever-changing scenes of great peace and beauty. The Churchtown, the main village of Quethiock, and the tiny hamlets of Blunts, to the east, and Trehunist to the west, are joined by winding lanes, mostly only of cart-width, across which may rush a tiny stream with a miniature clapper-bridge for the convenience of those on foot. For them also there is often a central ribbon of green grass, laid like a soft royal carpet that winds uphill and down. The farms, especially the larger ones, are almost all completely hidden from view down their own long lanes, for this is a very dispersed parish.

I remember being told by a St. Ive man, who was a small boy in the days when farm horses used to queue outside his father's smithy to be shod, that when the wait was likely to be a long one the farm workmen would leave their charges and get back to work. Later, after they had been shod, the small boy would lead the great, powerful creatures along to the end of their farm-lane, release them, and with a tap on their rears let them find their own way home.

Quethiock is also a parish of woodlands, its coppices and timber trees carefully preserved by generations of sporting Squires. The deciduous woods along the river banks are, even to this day, places of enchantment, full of flowers, ferns and wildlife, a paradise for children. The proportion of woodland has always been high. At the time of the Tithe Apportionment in 1842 there were 307 acres of woodland in the parish as compared with only 472 acres of meadowland and pastureland combined.

*The family which outgrew their little village shop at 'Ferndale' and for whom the 'new shop' was specially built. The two youngest children, Winnie and Donald, were born there, the rest at the earlier shop 'Ferndale'. Front, left, is Louis Harris, mentioned in Chapter 7, who died in 1973, aged 89. Next to him is Jenny, now 86 (1977). Dainty little Hetty, standing between her mother and father, never married but Effie, like Jenny, married a farmer. The two boys, on the right, emigrated to Australia Tom, back row, came home on a visit but Charles, front, never returned. Eugene, by his mother, took over the shop. Will, back row left, is remembered on the War Memorial.*

*Enter bureaucracy and the 'infernal' combustion engine! Mr. Harold Hosking, Surveyor for the newly formed (1894) St. German's Rural District Council at the wheel of his 12hp. Darracq, Registration number AF 911. Mr. Joseph Bate, carpenter, of Lower Pounda is the elder of the passengers. Behind them are Well Cottages, home of George Riddle.*

At that time of high farming the arable acreage was 2529 acres of rich, easily-tillable land with good drainage. Quethiock was therefore fertile, well-watered, well-wooded and extremely beautiful. The Cornwall County Council fully appreciated, and was ready to pay a high price for, the first three attributes. Perhaps even the last was appreciated by any County Councillors who visited the parish, but not, I think, the tragic social consequences of their action.

Here, when they first saw it, was a rural community of the traditional close-knit kind, its corporate social and working life still almost intact, a territory organised for many centuries for agricultural production, occupied entirely by country people headed by their Squire, himself a wise and active countryman. In 1919 here lived the traditional primary population of tenant-farmers and husbandmen (to use the fine old word for the workmen) and the secondary one of all those who served their needs, both physical and spiritual, — the parson, schoolmaster, village shopkeeper, publican, and all the craftsmen. This extremely self-contained village community had only recently lost its own tailor and shoemaker, and the parish two of its millers. But it still employed blacksmiths, carpenters, woodmen and gamekeepers, also a mason, miller and wheelwright. The wheelright, Sidney Hawken of Treweese Cross, last of a long line of skilled craftsmen, made handsome farm carts and waggons. (We still treasure one of ours, both beautiful and soundly constructed about 75 years ago, with our name and the parish proudly painted in blue.)

Even in 1919 the parish, though certainly not rich in money, was still able to satisfy the human aspirations, and the human spirit of its people by offering pride in a variety of skilled crafts and even a possibility of advancement in agriculture for those able men and women prepared to work extra hard, this because of the great variety of size of holdings and the ease of renting land. The parish also offered a surprisingly full and varied social life, as we shall see. Because there is no continuity between the traditional close-knit community which began to collapse soon after the Sale, and the Quethiock of today, it is difficult to imagine that old leisurely, collective type of farming which was such an obstacle to the introduction of the modern competitive commercial industry; difficult also to remember that the much rarer leisure hours were largely occupied by productive and creative pursuits like gardening, dressmaking and music-making; perhaps most difficult of all to imagine a whole parish in which there really was social unity, for the simple reason that everyone's status, from Squire to cottager, their duties and their rights, were clearly defined and always had been, time out of mind. The social order was undoubtedly stratified but totally accepted. As one studies the Quethiock marriage registers, where the occupations of the fathers of both bride and groom are stated, one notes that the sons of the yeomen, the more substantial farmers, usually marry the daughters of other yeomen, farmer's sons marry farmer's daughters and the craftsmen marry among themselves, millers to blacksmiths, sawyers to carpenters, and so on. Lastly, the husbandmen, as the farm workers were always described until the second half of the 19th century, almost invariably married the daughters of other husbandmen. There were very few exceptions. Yet in spite of this quite rigid social stratification there was also real social unity, a lack of envy, a contentment with one's station in life that we find so incomprehensible today. What explained it?

The most important factor, I suggest, was that all the Squire's tenants, from the largest to the smallest, knew that under the Corytons their possession of land was secure, that if their sons were good and capable farmers they would be able to take over the tenancy of the family farm without question. Rents were low, and in difficult times could be, and often were, lowered for everyone. For all there was hope of advancement. No-one envied the Squire with his great responsibilities, not even the cottagers. They could rent as much land as they could cultivate, cheaply, and with an equal measure of security. I shall describe how a hard-working and efficient young married man with a good wife could, and did, rise from being a farm labourer with a plot of land to the status of a yeoman farmer. Even those cottagers who never rose in the social scale, provided that they had a cow — road-side grazing was common — a few pigs, some poultry and an abundant supply of fruit and vegetables, were unlikely to go hungry. I am certain that from the 1880's onward no-one in Quethiock ever did go hungry. Of course, ample food production was hard work, hard slogging work for women and children as well as men, but it brought a sense of real achievement as well as friendly rivalry and a community of interests. When one looks at the immensely long list of local prize-winners at the Quethiock Flower and Horticultural Shows around the turn of the century it is difficult to remember that the population of the whole parish at that time was only about 430 persons (later, by 1961, to have decreased to 317, the lowest ebb).

These four-hundred people were extremely self-sufficient, not only in the production of their own food, but in their use of other local resources, stone, wood, wheat-straw for thatching and water for power. Their demands upon outside resources were exceedingly small, as I discovered when I began to study our old Quethiock farm account books. Here was a society engaged in production, not consumption, not one being everlastingly cajoled to get into debt, with the carrots of increased monetary profit, or of social esteem, as the rewards. In fact, from the Squire down to the humblest cottager, no-one was solely activated by the prospect of profit. Moreover social esteem could not be purchased. Hire purchase was unknown and farmers usually were able to borrow money, if they needed it, within the family. Connections by marriage formed a dense parish network. My husband's paternal grandparents each came from families of eleven children, so from them alone he was probably related to three quarters of the old parish. Neighbourly help was also swiftly forthcoming for genuine misfortune. I was told the tale of one small farmer whose one and only precious rick of hay had been burned to the ground. In those days there was no insurance. The parish rallied around. Carts and wagons came creaking up his lane all bearing loads of good-quality hay and he finished up with twice the amount of hay as had been in the lost rick.

Thrift was a very highly valued virtue and nothing was bought until the money had been saved to pay for it. The modern money-lenders' siren-song, "Take the waiting out of wanting", would have been totally incomprehensible to men and women brought up to shun debt like the plague. A very popular song in Cornwall at the turn of the century was entitled, "Measure your wants by your means", which was sung at many a Quethiock concert to enthusiastic applause. This song expressed local sentiment perfectly. The people of the parish were self-reliant folk, certainly not the 'dim, sad, small figures dwarfed by space and sky' as imagined by urban intellectuals. No, in spite of their long hours of work, in spite of the famous Quethiock rain and infamous Quethiock mud, they could still play all manner of practical jokes upon one another, could still laugh uproariously without having to get drunk first, and when a group got together, could still sing for joy, and in perfect harmony. My photographs show people that are neither dim, sad, nor small, but alert, jolly and on the tall side, while the women and children are often lovely.

This was the parish community whose fate was decided on August 14th, 1919, but which fortunately had been recorded in great detail, as far as its infrastructure was concerned, in the fine and detailed Brochure prepared for likely buyers. This is a perfect and detailed blueprint of a traditional rural parish as it had existed for many centuries, drawn before men and horses had largely been replaced by machines, while the village cottages were still occupied by farm workmen and while the craftsmen were still busy in their workshops. There were good, clear photographs of every farmhouse, together with an exact description of each, inside and out, and of all the farm buildings. Although the smaller properties had not been photographed they too were all described in equal detail. The brochure even described kitchen and dairy equipment, and one learned that every farmhouse had its apple room, and some a cider press, while there was a community cider-press in the village. Three splendid maps came with the brochure, one of them a large-scale ($\frac{1}{1250}$, based on O.S.) map of the village, showing all its farms, cottages, and other dwellings, including outhouses, and the gardens and vegetable plots. Fascinating as it was, on to the dry bones of the old brochure I now longed to see flesh, I wanted to meet some of the people who had lived and worked there before the great dispersal, and hear what they had to say about their parish.

*An ever welcome visitor to Quethiock. Nurse Burton, from the South Devon & East Cornwall Hospital at Plymouth, who nursed Harry Riddle through a dangerous illness in 1902.*

*One of the Pentillie Estate woodmen and part-time gamekeeper with his family. He looks rather grim but his charming little daughter could, no doubt, wind him around her little finger.*

# The Squires

"Happy the Parish that has a Good King" (John Scott 1773)

The most important attribute of Squire William Coryton, for the people of Quethiock, was not that he came of ancient lineage and was an inheritor of fine traditions nor that he was a large landowner who lived in considerable state in an imposing mansion, but that he was a countryman to his fingertips, one whose work, responsibilities and pleasures lay almost entirely in his native westcountry. Thus his relationship with them was far more than the simple landlord-tenant one of modern times. It was personal and all-embracing. Naturally it included all the tenant farmers who, bound by the strict terms of their leases, were expected to make good husbandry their first consideration. It also included the woodmen who cared for coppices and timber, the gamekeepers, water-bailiffs, and all the craftsmen in stone, wood and iron. It included the schoolmaster and the schoolchildren, the villagers and the Vicar. Squire William not only insisted upon good sound husbandry and good sound workmanship, using local resources wherever possible, but he would ride many miles to see work in progress. This personal concern and personal contact was one reason why Quethiock remained a happy parish, its social fabric intact, long after many other rural areas had sunk into sloughs of poverty and hopelessness.

The Coryton lineage is important because eighty years ago real deference was still paid to 'the gentry', as had been the case from time immemorial. This was by no means a thoughtless deference. Every country clod-hopper knew the difference between the 'real gentry' and those upstart buyers of estates, no matter how powerful and wealthy, whose pedigrees were unknown. Deference was something that could not be bought, and in those days it was very real.

Coming originally from the Manor of Coryton in Devon, where the family had been established, according to 'Burke's Landed Gentry', some time before the Conquest, a Jefferie Coryton came to Cornwall about 1242 and married Isolda, daughter and heiress of John de Ferras of West Newton in St Mellion parish, only a stone's throw from Quethiock across the river Lynher. Thereafter Newton Ferras became the family seat for some four hundred years which explains why the Coryton monuments are in St Mellion church. Against the north wall of the chancel is a Monumental Brass to Peter Coryton, who died in 1551, and his widow, Jane, who died in 1558. Under their effigies are depicted all their children, seventeen sons and seven daughters. Peter Coryton wears a hauberk, a tunic of chain mail, over his plate armour, Jane a long gown and a triangular head-dress. There are other elaborate monuments to Corytons, particularly those of the seventeenth and eighteenth centuries. Now there is no more room for burials inside the church and the Squire with whom I am most concerned is buried in the churchyard and commemorated by a very simple headstone.

It was while they lived at Newton Ferras that the Corytons acquired the manor of Trehunsey, in Quethiock, anciently the home of the Kingdons. Trehunsey became Coryton property by two stages, both involving lucrative marriages to heiresses. First the manor came to the Chiverton family through marriage with a Kingdon heiress, and then secondly from the Chivertons to the Corytons by the marriage of

Elizabeth, daughter and co-heiress of Sir Richard Chiverton, to Sir John Coryton, who was born in 1648 and died in 1690, and was the second baronet. In 1739, through lack of a male heir, the baronetcy became extinct and the family seat, Newton Ferras, was claimed by the childless widow of Sir John Coryton, the fourth baronet. However much other property was regained by a suit-at-law and Peter Goodall, a second cousin, now became the head of the family, assumed the name of Coryton, (his grandmother's maiden name) and came to live at Crocadon, St Mellion.

The family, however, were not destined to live here for very long. Soon came yet another fortunate marriage, this time of John Coryton, son of Peter, b. 1740, with Mary Jemima, only child and sole heiress of James Tillie of Pentillie Castle, Pillaton, near Saltash. The fascination of male Corytons for heiresses is said to have provoked this couplet:—

"Refuse noe woman ne'er so old,
Whose marriage bringeth store of gold."

After the marriage between John and Mary Jemima, Pentillie Castle became the family seat and remains so to this day. One point to add, to what can only be a brief sketch of such a long family history, is that the Corytons were by no means mere country squires. For example, William Coryton, born in 1579, Vice-Warden of the Stannaries of Cornwall from 1603-30, a parliamentary Member for the County and a friend of Hampden, Pym and Elliott, with them resisted forced loans and arbitrary powers. He strongly supported the Petition of Right and was among those imprisoned for having forcibly detained the Speaker in the Chair. Another William, Sir William, 3rd Bt, was M.P. for Callington in no less than four reigns, that of Charles II, James I, William III, and Queen Anne. However, as I am chiefly concerned with the Corytons in their role as Squires of Quethiock, I must turn to more immediate and local traditions.

Colonel Augustus Coryton (1809-1891), the Uncle of William Coryton (1847-1919), lived unmarried at Pentillie Castle for over fifty years together with his sister, Miss Charlotte. He was a fine example of a Good King to all his parishes, a lenient landlord as far as rents were concerned, but always insistent upon good husbandry. Both he and his sister were staunch supporters of the churches and schools in his domain, including those of Quethiock. His style of living was entirely in the old grand tradition. Here, for example, is an account of the Pentillie festivities that brought the year 1884 to a close, and one which would have been read in *The Cornish Times* with tremendous local interest.

### Seasonable Festivities at Pentillie Castle

Christmas and the advent of the New Year have been observed at Pentillie Castle in the usual good old English style. During the week preceding Christmas the coverts were shot, resulting in an ample supply of pheasants and hares which were liberally distributed among the tenantry and others in the neighbourhood. Colonel Coryton's annual gifts in money and coals have also been distributed to the poor of the neighbouring parishes. Miss Coryton's entertainment for the schoolchildren in Christmas week consisted of a capital Punch and Judy exhibition from Plymouth, followed by a substantial tea, concluding with an excellent imitation of waxworks by amateurs of the neighbourhood. Over 100 children were present and were highly delighted with the entertainment and the performances. The mechanics and labourers employed on the estate were, with their wives, entertained at dinner in the spacious Hall of the Castle, the party numbering 96, when full justice was done to the abundant supply of Christmas beef and pudding, and the real malt and hop ale brewed on the premises. A professional from Plymouth led off the appropriate songs after the various toasts, and also furnished the music for the dancing that followed.

William Coryton, imperturbable Victorian squire, who enjoyed a peaceful Sunday afternoon in his study after a busy week. On one such occasion, in April 1904, his equanimity was shattered when he received an urgent message. King Edward VII was even then proceeding upstream, in a launch, and would like to visit Pentillie. A family conference, about suitable clothes, was held at once. Fortunately the squire's wedding trousers still fitted and his wife produced a frock coat, unworn, that she had bought him (she always maintained he would only wear it at her funeral to please her!) while his butler-valet produced a top hat. Thus garbed he went forth to meet his King who later expressed his delight at the visit.

This engraving of Pentillie Castle, as it appeared in Victorian days, shows its superb situation high on a wooded bank on the Cornish side of the River Tamar. Its name has derived from a battlemented house built by Sir James Tillie who died in 1712 and was by him thus denominated. It became the Coryton family seat after John Coryton, of Crocadon (see text) married the sole Tillie heiress, Mary Jemina. Their son, John Tillie Coryton, rebuilt the castle to the design of W. Wilkins, Esq., who also designed King's College, Cambridge. Although enlarged in 1810, the additional wings were demolished in 1968 and the present building is smaller than depicted here.

On February 17th 1887 the *Western Morning News* announced a marriage.

> At the pretty little church of Cornwood yesterday were solemnised the nuptials of Mr William Coryton, eldest son of the late Mr George Edward Coryton, of Liss, Hants, and nephew of Colonel Coryton of Pentillie Castle, and Miss Evelyn Annie Parker, second daughter of Admiral Parker of Delamore, Cornwood.

followed by an account of the festivities.

> In celebration of the marriage of Mr William Coryton with Miss Evelyn Parker, Colonel Coryton gave all his employees a holiday, and for the amusement of those inclined for outdoor sport he allowed them the run of his preserves for ferreting and shooting rabbits. In the evening the spacious rooms at the Castle were placed at the disposal of the servants and their friends for a ball . . . and the party consisted of nearly one hundred. Music was supplied by the St Germans Quadrille Band, and dancing was kept up until the small hours of the morning.
>
> More than a hundred other employees were invited to a feast at St Mellion schoolroom.

The following year the same paper announced another event under Births: "Coryton. August 25th at Hatt, East Cornwall, the wife of William Coryton, of a son."

In its issue of September 9th, 1891. *The Western Morning News* announced the death, in his 82nd year, of Col. Coryton.

> Col. Coryton, the warm-hearted owner of Pentillie Castle, died at his beautiful mansion on the banks of the River Tamar on Monday evening. Col. Coryton was born in 1809, the eldest surviving son of John Tillie Coryton.
>
> Col. Coryton paid much attention to agriculture and during his long life did much to improve the estate. At one time he was farming 1,500 acres and it was a part of his system, as the holdings fell into his hands, to retain them and improve the land before letting it to other tenants. In this way he rendered much rough and unprofitable soil highly productive.
>
> He was a staunch Churchman and a liberal supporter of his own communion. He held always that it was the duty of a land-owner to contribute generously towards the maintenance of the church fabric and he furnished ample evidence of the sincerity of this conviction when, 10 or 11 years ago, he contributed from £1,500 to £2,000 towards the restoration of Quethiock Church, in which parish he owned the bulk of the land.
>
> He subscribed to various County charities, but his private benefactions were distributed by no niggard hand.
>
> He was careful always to make provision for those who had served him faithfully and well, and a large number of pensioners in the neighbourhood of Pentillie were indebted to him for an easy existence during the decline of life.
>
> The coffin was of oak grown on the estate, and was made by the Head Carpenter. The Head Gardener at Pentillie, complimented upon his flower arrangements for the funeral, said "It was a labour of love; it was the last service I could render to the dear old Master."
>
> The Coryton family were far more than good masters and mistresses — they were good friends to all about them. This feeling that had arisen between master and man, and tenant and landlord, ran through the whole family, so that there was a feeling amongst them of the proverbial faggot — if they put them across their knees they could not break them.

Miss Charlotte Coryton died in 1897, aged 79, and many tributes were paid to her also, saying that her long life had been one of great service to the whole neighbourhood. In 1842, with her sister, she had built the schools at Cross, was always a generous subscriber, and visited the school regularly once a week. Also she held a Sunday School there for many years, and also a night-school at Pentillie Quay. She originated the Cherry-Pie Feast at Pentillie, to which all the children of neighbouring parishes came, to feast upon ripe cherries and other delights. She was a pioneer spirit in the cause of education. Mr Harold Martin of St Mellion, born in 1893, remembers her well, coming in a phaeton to the school with a little white dog. In his last year at school Mr Martin had won a diploma for top marks, and was offered further free education at Truro from a fund set up by Miss Charlotte. Unfortunately the boy's labour was urgently needed on the family farm and he was unable to take advantage of it.

I myself have special reason to be grateful to Miss Charlotte. Every time I drive through St Mellion on my way to Plymouth I check my watch with the fine blue-and gold clock in the church tower. *The Western Morning News* of 25th October, 1894, reported:—

> Miss Coryton of Pentillie has formally handed over to the Rector "for the benefit of the parishioners" a magnificent church-turret clock. On a polished brass plate in the belfry is inscribed:—
>
> > This clock was given on Wednesday, October 24th, 1894 by Charlotte Coryton
> > of Pentillie Castle, for the benefit of the parishioners and in remembrance of the
> > many years she has worshipped God with them in this church.

One realises that William Coryton succeeded not only to a great estate but also to a fine tradition of service. The care for the land, the care for individual tenants and other parishioners, the care for churches and schools, all these were continued by the new Squire. Even the famous Pentillie balls continued as before. Here is an account of a ball held in 1893, from *The Western Morning News* of the 4th of January.

> The genial Squire of Pentillie, Mr William Coryton, gave the annual ball to the servants and their friends, about 80 in number, on Wednesday. The large company assembled, bent on thoroughly enjoying themselves. The large dining-room had been prepared for dancing, and about 9 o'clock the ball was opened by Mrs Coryton and Mr Jenkins, the butler, leading off with Sir Roger de Coverley. At the opposite end of the long string of dancers was Mrs Bushnell, the housekeeper, with the young Squire, Master J.T. Coryton as her partner.
>
> Dancing was kept up with great spirit until midnight, when an adjournment was made for supper to the great hall, which had been splendidly decorated by Mr Cove, the head gardener and his assistants.

The account of the ball continues with the healths drunk, and the speeches made after supper. Then followed a further long programme of dancing and music, which must have continued well into the small hours.

The celebration of Queen Victoria's Diamond Jubilee in 1897 was the occasion for great rejoicing in all the Coryton parishes. At St Mellion, for example, the day started with a cricket match, followed by a free meat tea in the Rectory grounds. This was followed in the evening by athletic sports at Cow-park, including

*The coming-age celebrations, at Pentillie Castle, on August 25th, 1909, when John Tillie Coryton, the heir, attained his majority. The ladies and gentlemen in the front row are members of the Coryton family and the heir sits between his mother and father. Behind them are ranks of the more substantial tenants and in all, some 600 tenants were sumptuously entertained that day.*

*This was the first car ever seen in Quethiock, AF 178, a Sunbeam registered by W. Coryton on August 8th, 1906. It had come to the village to pick up members of a shooting party who were taking late refreshments at East Quethiock Farm. The villagers gathered around this new monster and hitherto accustomed to trap-lamps were astounded by the powerful headlights.*

pony-racing. At 10.00 p.m. a capital bonfire was lit on Viverdon Down. The scene was a most impressive one as on hill after hill, from Dartmoor to Roche, the beacon lights flared up. Then there were fireworks, and torch-bearers lit the homeward route. Supper followed in the Schoolroom and dancing went on till the small hours.

The highest point of festivities at Pentillie, certainly for Quethiock folk, was the coming of age of the heir, John Tillie Coryton, on August 25th 1909. I could find only one old gentleman from Quethiock who had actually been present on that splendid occasion as the eldest son of one of the biggest farmers in the parish. Alas, all he could remember about the great day was the food, enormous tables laden with unbelievable quantities of delicious food, in such wonderful variety as a small boy of eleven would remember for the rest of his long life. Fortunately I could find a full account of the day's happenings in *The Cornish Times* of Friday, August 22nd, together with a large photograph of the heir. Here are some extracts:—

The Pentillie Heir Coming-of-Age Celebrations at the Castle

The Tenantry Entertained

Mr John Tillie Coryton, the eldest son and heir of Mr William Coryton of Pentillie Castle attained his majority on Wednesday.

The young Squire has become intimately acquainted with the whole of the tenantry. He is of a most genial disposition and has, like his father, the sporting blood running strong in his veins, being an ardent follower of the hounds and a lover of the gun. The tenants all recognise in him one whom they can trust to follow in the footsteps of his father.

Nearly 600 of the tenantry and their wives, and employees, partook of the lavish hospitality extended to them. They came from the parishes of St Mellion, Quethiock, St Dominick, St Ive, Callington, Colebrooke, (N.Devon) and the employees of the Three Towns Dairy Co., Plymouth. The dairy employees came from Plymouth by water. There was dancing on the green to music supplied by the Saltash Territorial Band. The sumptuous luncheon and tea were served in a marquee on the terrace.

Mr John Braund of Calstock said that he well remembered Miss Elizabeth and Miss Charlotte Coryton who would come out in all weathers with their grey donkey and little white dog to teach him and the other children on a Sunday afternoon. He knew the present Squire as well as most men did. They ought to be proud of him. No man could be a better landowner. It would have been a poor day for some of the tradesmen in that neighbourhood if it had not been for their present squire, for when the mining was at its lowest ebb he had the pluck to spend his money, and kept scores of families that would otherwise have had no bread.

The Squire was a noble father. He hoped that the son would prove a noble son.

Mr Braund then presented the young Squire with a silver table centre-piece for flowers and fruit inscribed

Presented to John Tillie Coryton

by the tenantry of the Pentillie estates

on his coming of age.

25th August 1909

Many other presentations followed, including a silver-mounted toilet outfit from the household servants and presented by Mr C Jenkins, butler for 24 years.

*This fine oil painting of William Coryton hangs on [...] Pentillie Castle. It was presented to him in June 1901 b[y] the Dartmoor Hunt of which he had been Master sin[ce...] William was extremely proud of his hounds and esp[ecially] strong feet, so essential in this wild, rough country, a[nd] requested the artist "to keep the grass short".*

*rcase at
ribers to
. Squire
of their
herefore*

One gazes at the photographs taken on this happy day with astonished sadness. Here sits the handsome young heir with his mother and his father on each side, and with other members of his family in the front row; behind him row upon row of the farm tenants rise in tiers, solid men all, including my husband's grandfather, his father, and several other members of his family on both sides. Did any of them know that in Europe the storm clouds were already gathering? They knew, of course, that the young heir was about to embark on a military career, and join the Rifle Brigade. What they could not know was that he was to be severely wounded in the First World War and that his heir, Peter Coryton, was to be killed in the Second.

It all looks so stable, so permanent, that we can hardly persuade ourselves of the truth of the inscription on the Quethiock sundial, "So soon passeth it away".

The Pentillie tradition of lavish hospitality was still being faithfully observed, so was another, a farming tradition. William Coryton followed his uncle in his enthusiasm for progressive farming. *The Western Daily Mercury* of May 18th, 1898 reports:—

> Mr Coryton farms a considerable portion of the estate lying around Pentillie for dairy purposes, his herd of milch cows (South Devon and Jersey) numbering about 288. Necessarily this entails a tremendous amount of work and the employment of a large staff to cope with the obtaining, treatment and despatch of 500 gallons of milk per day . . . to supply The Three Towns Dairy and its branches, which Mr Coryton has established.

The following year the same paper notes that

> . . . only tuberculin-tested milk is now supplied to The Three Towns Dairy, the first time that tuberculin testing has been applied to such an extent.

The story of the enclosure and ploughing of Viverdon Down, the latter a task that would be a formidable one even with modern machinery, was begun in 1893 and continued into the next century. Some 650 acres of virgin land, mostly culm, were cleared, drained, ploughed, and then again cleared of the stones thrown up by the plough. The monster ploughs used were ordered, and specially made, by John Drown, an agricultural implement maker of St Mellion. James Jane, the carpenter at Blunts made the templates for them. The work was undertaken by a small army of men, and many teams of horses, six to a team for ploughing, with three waggoners to each team, for the work was extremely hard. Many men had been thrown out of work by the closing of the Devon Great Consols Mine. This was Squire William's solution. He hated to see willing men idle. There was plenty of work for them here. First the gorse and scrub must be cleared and tied into faggots, later to be placed over the land drains, five feet down. The ploughing threw up immense quantities of stones so a great number of men picked them up and sorted them for size, the smallest to be put over the faggots in the drains, the larger ones for hedge-building, and the rest for road-making. Miles of hedges must be constructed, and gates made from estate timber. When Squire Coryton had drained the Down, some of which had hitherto been no better than bogland, he utilised the water by raising it, with two rams and a wind mill, to the highest part, where it filled two large reservoirs. From these it flowed back to many field water-troughs and to farms and cottages.

What is particularly note-worthy about the whole operation is that it was carried out from a single room in the Estate Office. Paper work, once the Enclosure Scheme had satisfied Commoner's rights and Local Authority requirements, must have been kept at an absolute minimum. Yet everything went smoothly over all the natural obstacles. There was, however, an obstacle of a different kind. There remains a small part of Viverdon Down still in its original state, except for a little drainage. Here the work of reclamation was stopped abruptly when Lloyd George, then Chancellor of the Exchequer, decided to levy a tax on Enclosures. Squire William, having battled with bogs, black-ram and flint-stones at considerable personal expense, decided that enough was enough. The tax was the last straw. He quit, and this piece of wasteland is ironically called "Lloyd George's Ground" to this day.

While the reclamation of Viverdon Down was Squire William's largest scheme to combat mass unemployment he had many others. Elsewhere many more miles of stone hedges were built to his strict specifications and stand, sturdy and perfect, as a testimony to his oversight. He ordered the construction of many 'passing places' in narrow lanes. He ordered the building of many new farmhouses, farm buildings and other dwellings. For example, Quethiock's well-built Village Stores-cum-Post Office bears his initials and the date 1897. His initials and the date were branded on all the farm gates which were made on the estate from home-grown timber. It was quite usual for them to last for fifty years, and a few are still in use today. Those made for Viverdon Down were five-barred gates, nine feet long, with oak gateposts one foot square, and were constructed entirely without nails, only with wooden pegs and bolts. One can still see Squire William's initials on a great many cast-iron well-heads, for, where there was no water available to be brought to farms by gravitation, he ordered the deepening and re-lining of wells. In all these many activities he showed tremendous organising ability, ably assisted by his bailiff, John Petherick, who was a considerable character in his own right, and notorious for driving a jingle at a furious pace. One day, so the story goes, the Squire challenged his bailiff to a race from Holwood, in Quethiock, back to Paynter's Cross at Pentillie, the Squire on horseback, the bailiff in his jingle. However John Petherick was suspicious. Squire might be tempted to jump a few hedges and take some short cuts. So he agreed to the race provided that they both carried an egg in each coat pocket which must be unbroken at the finish. Squire William was first home with both eggs broken; John Petherick, with both his eggs intact, won the day.

The St Germans Rural District Council, newly created in 1894, was also ready with a challenge. *The West Briton and Cornwall Advertiser* of September 23rd, 1897, carried this item:—

St Germans. Alleged nuisance at Cargreen.

At St Germans Rural District Council meeting yesterday a letter was read calling attention to the unloading of a barge of refuse at Cargreen. The objectionable refuse belonged to Mr Coryton, the refuse having been taken from the kennels and stables at Ivybridge. The stench was very bad. The stuff was carted through the village and got littered about. Discussion took place as to whether a summons should be issued against Mr Coryton . . . but it was agreed eventually that this should be left to the discretion of the Clerk.

No doubt the Clerk wrote a firm, but civil letter to Mr Coryton, and no doubt a less offensive way was found to bring "the stuff" back to enrich the soil of Pentillie for no more was heard of the matter. On another occasion the Squire was criticised for the lack of cottage accommodation in St Dominick, and was requested to build some new ones. This he did, for three years later *The Cornish Times* in 1898 was able to report that all was now well, adding:—

In every respect Mr Coryton appears to be doing his best to improve his property in the district and provide the required accommodation for tenants and work-people. It is by no means generally known how close and keen an interest Mr Coryton personally takes in the domestic lives of his tenants . . .

The people of Quethiock knew. As I was gathering material for this book I was told many stories of his past kindness, remembered with gratitude to this day. In his concern for individual people Squire William was only following yet another strong family tradition. Here is just one example, from many that I heard

*The draining and ploughing of Viverdon Down began in 1898 in order to provide desperately needed work for displaced Cornish miners (see text) and continued for ten years. The land was stony culm so three waggoners and six horses were needed to each strong, and locally made, plough. The man on the left is picking up stones which were graded and used for drains, hedges and roads.*

*Hayricks being made at the entrance to Dunston Farm. This fine crop is being gathered late in the year on land drained and reclaimed by Squire William. Note the drainage pipes inside the hedge, on the left. Because of Lloyd George's tax on enclosures the scheme was never quite completed.*

from the families concerned. As a young farm lad James Jane, of Blunts, was paring nettles in a field when he was tossed by a bull and one of his legs was broken. It set badly and James' future as a farm worker seemed poor, for farming in those days meant miles of rough walking. William Coryton, hearing about the lad's accident and its unfortunate sequel, made arrangements for him to be apprenticed to a good carpenter. When James' time had been served successfully, the Squire, in 1890, on William Coryton's advice (he was not to inherit the estate until the following year, and the Squire was Colonel Augustus Coryton) built a carpenter's shop for him at Blunts, close to his father-in-law Bennett's smithy. Thus, in *Venning's Directory of East Cornwall* published in 1901 one can read the proud entry:—

> Jane, James. Carpenter and Smith. Blunts

The Coryton generosity could move from the particular to the general, especially when times were really hard for the farmers. From time to time an announcement such as this, made at Michaelmas 1895, would appear in the local press:—

> At the Pentillie Rent Audit held at Callington, Liskeard and Quethiock during the past week Mr Coryton again allowed his farm tenants an abatement of 10% on their Michaelmas half-years rent.

Fortunate farmers, to be dealing with a man who understood their problems because he was himself a farmer and not with an anonymous financial organisation that must, come what may, get its pound of flesh!

Traditional in all else — in his hospitality, his progressive farming, his concern for his people — William Coryton also was a traditional enthusiastic hunting and shooting squire. I hope, as he lay in his last illness, that he was able to remember the happy times that he had spent in Quethiock woods with his family and friends, or perhaps, in imagination, ride again with the famous Dartmoor Hunt of which he was so long Master. It is now fashionable to sneer at fox-hunters and give all one's sympathy to the poor fox. Country folk who keep sheep, and rear poultry, know that foxes are killers, not just killers for food but cruel killers for fun. Few farmer's wives who, like me, have found a heap of massacred point-of-lay pullets in a fowl-house with an insecurely shut pop-hole can ever feel over-sorry for the fox. Indeed, in tough hunting country like ours, and particularly on Dartmoor and Bodmin Moor, where bogs are frequent and the going heavy, one may sometimes have more sympathy with the riders. Often only a handful see the run through before the fox goes to ground, while most have come to grief on the way. Fox-hunting may be ritualised killing but at least it takes endurance, courage, physical fitness and perseverance. In former years *The Cornish Times* regularly published excellent accounts of local Meets. Here is one, dated January 19th, 1884:—

### Mr Coryton's Hounds

> A recent Meet was held at Wenmouth Cross, about the best in East Cornwall. We found Hammett in the possession of two old foxes — of different sexes of course — and first called on "my gentleman" who gave us a spin of ten minutes and then ran to ground but only to appear on the scene again during the latter part of the day. We now paid our respects to "my lady" and she proved one of the most fickle of her sex. She pointed first for Carbilla, then for Browngelly, and back over the Colliver Moors to where we found. Next she went down to St Neot and back, and then did somewhat the same round of country again.
>
> After a hard badgering run of 2½ hours she was killed within sight of her home earth.

William Coryton had brought his own pack of beagles from Hampshire in the '70's and subsequently hunted the East Cornwall country with harriers and foxhounds at his own expense for fourteen years. In 1889 he took the Mastership of the Dartmoor, one of the finest packs in the West of England, and was acknowledged to have hunted the wild country across the Tamar with conspicuous success. *The Western Morning News* in "Notes in the West" for June 7th, 1901 records:—

> Subscribers to the Dartmoor Hunt have presented Mr Coryton, the Master, with his portrait. It is on view at Messrs Harris's Gallery in George Street, Plymouth, today the 8th, for one day only, then will go to London.

This fine oil-painting now hangs in the staircase at Pentillie, the Master on horseback, his hounds around him, and behind him the open, unfenced moor.

William Coryton was an excellent shot and for many years westcountry newspapers, and sporting papers such as *The Field*, carried news of his triumphs.

> Mr. Coryton and a party of friends from Pentillie on 26th inst. shooting at Quethiock made the unprecedented bag for the time of year, especially as partridges this season are unusually strong and wild, of 52 brace of partridges, 23 brace of pheasants and 21 rabbits.
>
> *The Western Morning News.* October 29, 1893

> A bag of partridges which is a record for this county was made by Mr William Coryton and a party of friends on his estates near Holwood and Quethiock on Thursday of last week. Thanks in great measure to the friendly feelings of the tenant farmers, who zealously preserve the game on this property, Mr Coryton, in spite of most unfavourable weather, was enabled to make the fine bag of 120½ brace, not counting the birds that were picked up next day.
>
> *The Cornish Times*, September 29 1898

> A bag of 105 brace of partridges was made on the 29th ult. at Quethiock, Cornwall by Mr Coryton and five other guns. This meant a good walk, as driving in this country is impossible.
>
> *The Field*, October 8, 1904

I have been given permission by Major Jeffery Coryton, grandson of William Coryton, and present owner of Pentillie, to quote "A Lay of Pentillie", written by "Mr Prince" and now treasured in the family papers, a reminder of past fun and joy.

"Now Jenkins, call us early in the morning, do you hear?
For we must be at Quethiock before the day is clear!
So order breakfast early, and be sure and make a 'mem'
To bring the shaving water at four o'clock, a.m."

The morn broke cold and dreary, but punctually at four,
The faithful butler roused them by knocking at the door;
"God bless me! What's the matter?" they each in turn did cry,
"You've got to be at Quethiock before the sun is high!"

There was Coryton of Pentillie, the Master of our Hounds,
Crake, Glencross, Hawker, Littleton, names known where sport abounds,
And lastly Major Eden, a soldier brave and gay,
Who fires ten thousand cartridges a season so they say.

*A group of harvesters. The tall man, on the left, is probably Richard Stacey, leader of the team, chosen both by Squire William and by the men themselves. For the extra responsibility a team leader received an additional £1 per week and a Christmas bonus of £10, (plus the not inconsiderable honour).*

*"Cherry Pie", the annual feast for all the children on the Pentillie estates, initiated by Miss Charlotte Coryton who died in 1897. The event was held at the Castle when the famous Tamar Valley cherries were ripe. The Corytons greatly encouraged the planting of cherry trees, strawberries and other fruit in order to provide extra employment.*

> Now the master of Pentillie a mighty oath had sworn
> That he would make a record bag of partridges that morn!
> So he summoned all his keepers and he summoned all his men,
> He had ten wagons waiting to carry back the game!
>
> There's trusty Hall and Hendy, just come from Langdon Court,
> Whose owner fair rears pheasants there for Royal Prince's sport;
> There's an ambulance with nurses too — for naught's forgot they find —
> The game-cart's packed with stretchers to bring those left behind!
>
> "Who's now the hardest walker? Who'll be the right-hand gun?"
> Their faces blanch, they look askance, but answer is there none!
> At last there's one steps forward, out from their ranks he ran;
> "I'll take the post of honour! I'll be the right-hand man!"
>
> They sweep across the mangolds, they stride across the swedes,
> They race along the arrishes, they run o'er all the seeds;
> "Break over here!" is oft the cry, and dashing at the banks,
> With faces worn, hands scratched and torn, not one drops from the ranks.
>
> They scorned to pause for luncheon, they scorned to take a rest,
> "On, on" 's the cry, "For we must try to do our level best!"
> And sure enough that afternoon as six o'clock came round,
> Full 80 brace of partridges were laid out on the ground.
>
> Then who so pleased as Coryton, and who so glad as they,
> Who'd walked a hundred miles or so throughout the livelong day,
> And now in future ages will the story oft be told,
> How these good men did keep their oath like heroes brave of old!"

One of the few sportsmen still able to talk about those long-ago days is Mr George Coryton, born in 1889, the second son of William Coryton and Uncle of Major Jeffery Coryton. He remembers that in the year 1907 Quethiock suffered from a plague of rabbits. A massive drive was organised, to include sportsmen, gamekeepers, farmers, and anyone else who could kill rabbits. No less than 14,000 were caught in the parish in that one year alone, and in the following year 7,000. They were sent off to Plymouth and Devonport markets in big wicker hampers, hanging upside-down in pairs. The price was sixpence each, of which half went to the farmer on whose land they were caught.

Mr George Coryton also can tell an amusing tale of a cunning fellow who lived in, or else near, Warren House Farm, the only farm in the parish which never belonged to the Corytons. This farm is close to Clapper Bridge over the River Lyhner and is surrounded by woodlands. The crafty villain used to catch Coryton gamebirds in substantial numbers by feeding them regularly inside a large wire-netting enclosure. Gradually the size of the enclosure would be reduced until one day — snap! — it was closed altogether. The trapped birds were then quietly removed and were seen no more. Mr George Coryton also mentioned that Quethiock had always been a famous place for hares and that the village children would always note where a hare was sitting so that they could inform the Harriers and claim a reward, just as they were rewarded when they found a nest of pheasant eggs.

One has to concede that Squire William's passion for hunting and shooting gave a great deal of enjoyment to his relatives and friends as well as employment to a large number of local people, grooms, kennelmen, foresters, gamekeepers and the like. His sporting activities also brought immense life and colour to Quethiock, perhaps especially to the children, as I shall describe presently. He was an autocrat, again in the old tradition, but he was a just one. One old lady told me that as a small girl on a visit to an older brother, the Miller at Trecorme Mill, she was thrilled when a Pentillie shooting party came trooping into the Mill kitchen. It was a wet and wintry day and everyone was plastered with mud. Squire William following a few moments later, immediately ordered the whole party to clear out and shelter in a barn, adding that they should be ashamed to come into any woman's clean kitchen in that filthy state. There was no argument. Out they went. On another occasion, still remembered in Quethiock, one of his sons was sent home in disgrace from another shoot. Climbing over a hedge, the lad, in his excitement, forgot to 'break' his gun. It was a sharp, public discipline which, no doubt, the young man never forgot. I have already mentioned the Vosper family who had lived at Haye for generations. Thomas Vosper had a dog who would not only chase hares but was swift enough to catch and kill them. This news got to William Coryton's ears. To Thomas Vosper he delivered his ultimatum, "Either you shoot the dog or you quit the farm!" Presumably he was obeyed in this instance also for the Vospers remained at Haye until 1919.

I hope that this short account of William Coryton, his lineage, the traditions he inherited at Pentillie, particularly from his Uncle, Colonel Augustus Coryton, and from his aunt, Miss Charlotte, his undoubted competence as a progressive and successful farmer, and his enthusiasm and skill as a sportsman, will give a just and balanced picture of the last Squire of Quethiock. The announcement of his death in *The Cornish Times* of August 29th, 1919, was accompanied by this obituary:—

> A wide circle of friends in the West Country has heard with regret of the death of Mr William Coryton of Pentillie Castle, Cornwall on Wednesday, 27th August in his 72nd year . . .
>
> Deceased was a large land-owner. He had been a J.P., Deputy Lieutenant of Cornwall and Sheriff of Cornwall in 1902. He had succeeded his uncle, Colonel Coryton, in 1891, and became the owner of the famous Pentillie Estate.
>
> What Mr Coryton accomplished in the matter of cattle-rearing and the cultivation of land is well-known. Within a radius of four miles of the Castle 1,400 acres has been farmed. He delighted in South Devons and at one time possessed 600 milch cows of that breed. Most of the milk was disposed of in Plymouth through "The Three Towns Dairies, Ltd."
>
> Thanks to his initiative hundreds of acres of barren land were brought under cultivation at Viverdon Down and in recent years he spent large sums of money on drainage and water schemes, thus turning to good use land which had hitherto been considered almost valueless. In the valley near the Castle much of the land is utilised for fruit-farming. It is a wonderful transformation in the development of which deceased took the leading part.
>
> He started hunting in 1870 and had not missed a season, up to 1915, for 45 years. He hunted the East Cornwall country at his own expense for 14 years. When he took over the Mastership of the Dartmoor Foxhounds from his father-in-law, Admiral Parker of Cornwood, South Devon, he hunted the country without subscription for many years. In his retirement he was presented with a massive grandfather clock by Hunt followers in recognition of his great services.

For the parish of Quethiock the centuries-long reign of its Good Kings had ended.

*Members of the Jane family outside their cottage at Blunts. Mr James Jane was befriended by the Coryton family after an accident (see text). He and his wife reared nine children in this cottage. Bill Jane, the cheeky little boy standing next to his mother, still lives there (1977) and can be seen in his cosy parlour, among the "helpers" at the end of the book.*

*Tommy Marks, one of the Pentillie Estate masons, flanked by two inquisitive young Wenmoths.*

*The Wenmoths of Goodmerry in 1913. Their birth dates and longevity are detailed at the end of section 3. They are, left to right:*
*Back Row – Anne, Jim, Wilfred, Kate.*
*Seated – Richard, Fanny, Joseph, Flora.*
*Front – Bessie, Carrie.*

# The Larger Farms

In my attempt to portray William Coryton, last Squire of Quethiock, I could only rely upon items from contemporary newspapers and upon the reminiscences of old people who had known him. I myself, as far as I know, had never met a squire in my life until I called upon his grandson at Pentillie Castle. Therefore it came as a surprise to me to learn that a good squire could play such an important economic and ecological role in rural affairs. I suppose I vaguely imagined that, as a class, squires were a kind of medieval relic, rent-taking parasites, certainly not men who could perform a complex and valuable function. In this case I was wrong. The Squire of Quethiock was the guardian of soil fertility, conservator of woods and water, pioneer of modern animal husbandry, a man who willingly assumed considerable responsibility for the welfare of his tenants. Admittedly, I only read about these things, or was told about them. I often studied his photographs but none revealed the man himself, except to indicate that he could face a camera with composed gravity. He reminded me of those solemn Elizabethans who look straight at one from their dark oil paintings, enigmatic beings from a different world.

When I came to study photographs of Quethiock farmers and their families there was no mystery. I saw familiar faces, younger than when I had first seen them, but still the faces of men and women I had known for many years. So I can describe them at first hand; I know their way of life because I followed hard on their farming heels. I too have lived without main water or electricity and have had to cope with a draughty open fireplace and a smoky kitchen range. I too have had to tend the charred lamp-wicks every morning and put out the row of candlesticks every evening with the invariable reminder, "Last to bed, put out the lamp!" True, I was saved by the wonderful advent of the milk-lorry from the demanding daily task of butter-making, but I have, as a youngster, watched it being made often enough, and I can still make it for ourselves.

As regards the other farm-wife's tasks, the putting-away of pigs, the huge cook-ups for the crowd of hay and corn harvesters before the day of the baler and combine, these also fell to my lot. My early years as a farmer's wife were not so very different from life at the turn of the century. There was a great deal of hard work to be done, indoors and out. Indeed, I do not wish to appear sentimental about farm life. God knows, it has its exasperations, its worries, and even its tragedies. Farmers are always in the front line of taking risks, battling against the unpredictable elements and against all the ills that can afflict, and sometimes kill, valuable farm stock. For farmers there are no clean pavements, no street lights, no convenient shops or schools, and few holidays; instead there is mud, darkness at nightfall, and a badly-rewarded 7-day a week job. No, I have no shining stars in my eyes when I remember the time when farming truly was a way of life.

The great changes in farming practice came fairly late to the westcountry. The present owner of Holwood, Mr John Tamblyn, told me that when he came there in 1943 he brought with him eight horses and had but one tractor. Many of our Cornish farmhouses still lacked all modern conveniences until well after the Second World War. It needs therefore no great effort of the imagination to reconstruct the life that used to revolve around the kitchens and dairies, and the work carried out in stables, shippons, barns and fields.

Before I begin to describe Quethiock's farms and farmers in some detail I should first like to place them in a much wider context than simply that of their own parish. Rural historians will know that, during the whole of the period with which I am now concerned, our British farmers had their backs to the wall, forced into this defensive position by some of their own thrusting, profit-seeking countrymen. These latter were the men who had helped to finance and build the great American railway system, and had also pioneered the building of iron ships with powerful marine engines and refrigerated holds. American railways grew from 30,000 miles in 1860 to 193,000 miles in 1900. The Far West now opened up, vast prairies were ploughed for the first time, releasing the stored fertility of aeons. The first trickles of cheap imported wheat soon became a flood. The grain was cheap because it came from this fertile virgin land and also because it came from a country almost empty of humans by European standards. American farms, at this time, were increasing in number twice as fast as the population, in spite of steady immigration. In 1860 there had been two million farms, by 1900 there were getting on for six million, and America had become the world's leading food exporter.

Our farmers, however efficient, could not possibly compete with American prices. So our wheat acreage dropped from 3,672,000 acres in 1875 to 1,795,000 acres in 1895, and the proportion of imported to homegrown wheat rose from 50.5% to 76.9%. In those same twenty years the price of wheat was halved, from just under 50 shillings a quarter to just over 24 shillings. British land values were also halved, plummeting from a total capital value of £2,007 million to £1,001 million.

In his book, "The Economic Impact of America", The Hon. George Peel describes these events as, "... a convulsion without parallel in an industry so basic and essential as agriculture and in a country so old and stable as our own". Undoubtedly a disastrous blow had been struck at the countryside. The Royal Commission on Agriculture reported in 1897 that, "farmers had for the past twenty years received on average only 60% of the sums which were, in past days considered as ordinary and average profit". The nation as a whole obviously benefited from this cheap imported food, including meat as well as wheat. Imports of meat rose from 265,000 tons in 1875 to 1,672,000 tons in 1895, 80% of it coming from America. British exports of manufactured goods were no doubt helped by the lower wages which this cheap food made possible, and even the farm workers were marginally better off, but landlords and farmers were hard hit. This international background needs to be borne in mind in all that follows, for where a rural community still prospered, as in Quethiock up to 1919, it was only because of extra hard work by farm families, including women and children, by strict budgeting, by remarkable self-sufficiency and even by self-denial. It was important also that the landlord should be generous and prepared to share his tenants' financial difficulties, also that the farm workers should be hard working and loyal. Thus, because farming profits were deliberately depressed in order to provide the new factory workers with cheap food, the farmers had to tighten their belts and work harder for less return. Yet in spite of the adverse economic climate, they, and their still very poorly-paid workmen, often sang as they went about their work. I know this because I am old enough to have listened to them. What had they to sing about?

*A wedding group at Treweese. The bridegroom is Francis Samuel Roseveare, aged 45, son of William Roseveare, of Treweese, and his bride is Miss Mary Caroline Kelly, aged 28, of Trecorme. They were married at the Parish Church on February 24th, 1903.*

*Treweese, farmed by Mr William Roseveare for many years. This photograph appeared in the Parish Magazine of July, 1900 and was again taken by the Vicar. Two Roseveare brothers and two sisters lived here, unmarried, until the 1919 sale.*

swiftly which of the cats were privileged house cats and which barn cats, for the latter would slink in like shadows given half a chance. Dogs were more law-abiding and accepted human judgement; one or two were house dogs, the others yard dogs.

The farm buildings were ranged around the yard, and with some gates, formed an enclosure called the town-place. They were built of the same grey stone and slate as the house. Many were of two storeys with flights of outside granite steps leading up to lofts and barns. The stables, four to six stalls or more, with a couple of loose boxes and a harness room were always situated close to the house. The reason was that the very first morning job after gulping down a hasty cup of tea and, except in high summer, lighting a lantern, was to get out to the stables and feed the horses, after they had been turned out for water. Working horses needed thorough daily grooming with curry-comb and brush, or sweaty shoulders could very soon become sore. The milking shippon was another building close to the house, partly because milking was yet another very early morning task, and partly to avoid carrying full buckets of milk any further than necessary, to the dairy or separator house.

Butter-making, so essential a part of Quethiock's farms in earlier days, has rarely been described in much detail, perhaps because it was an indoor job carried out in the early morning by one or two women, an inescapable daily routine task which everyone took for granted. However, because of its former importance, and also because butter-making is such a fine example of the sheer hard work performed by farm women I should like to do so.

Butter-making, perhaps I should explain, was revolutionised during the years leading up to the First World War by the gradual introduction of the separator, invented in 1878 by a Swede, Carl Laval. Before the introduction of the separator, pans of fresh milk had to be strained and then set to cool so that the ream* would rise. Next day this ream would be skimmed off, poured into a wooden tub and turned into butter simply by the swishing hands and forearms of the butter-maker. This was exceedingly hard work, for butter can take a perversely long time to 'come', often more than half an hour, and the swishing had to be continuous. After the turn of the century most farms with a large herd of milch cows, large that is by the standards of those days when all must be milked by hand, had bought a separator and so it is butter-making with separator and butter-churn that I shall now describe.

Quethiock's cows were all dual-purpose South Devons at this time, the large orange-brown native breed that has now been almost ousted by the Friesian, more's the pity! The South Devons gave fine rich milk, high in butter-fat. Twice daily, after milking, the buckets of fresh milk were brought to the house and strained into a 4-gallon bin from which it flowed slowly into the separator. By turning a handle the ream was separated from the rest of the raw milk and flowed into special gallon cream-cans with handles. These handles enabled the cans to be carried to a well or spring to cool, because butter could only be made satisfactorily from cool ream. This meant that in warm weather many farmer's wives and their maidservants had to trudge across fields to the nearest spring, carrying their gallon-cans, and then fetch them back again in the cool of early morning. The butter-churn into which the cool ream was now tipped was a tightly-lidded wooden tub with a small glass window and a handle. As one rocked the handle, which had to be done continuously and rhythmically, one could watch the ream rotating inside. After a while the first welcome globules of fat would appear on the glass and finally, quite suddenly there would be a bumping sound, the butter had 'come' and was now separated from the butter-milk. But this was by no means the end, now came the really skilled part, for every drop of liquid must be beaten out of the butter or it would not keep and would soon acquire a rancid flavour. A few farms had a little butter-mangle to hasten this process but the butter still had to be salted, and washed and pounded over and over and over again until it was dry, solid, and a lovely golden. Finally it was patted, with two butter-pats, into blocks or circles and after weighing, proudly stamped with the farm's special stamp.

On most Quethiock farms clotted cream was also made and sold. This involved much carrying of heavy pans of milk from dairy to scalding room and then back again. To make this scalded Cornish cream the pans

---

\* Westcountry term for raw, not clotted, cream.

of raw milk were allowed to settle for twenty-four hours until the ream had risen. Then the pan was lowered into a slightly larger pan containing very hot water and slowly heated to just below boiling point. If the cream boiled it was ruined. A solid crust of yellow cream would gradually develop, and when the farmer's wife judged it to be ready the pan was lifted from the hot water and taken back to the cool dairy. The following day the cream would be firmly set and was skimmed off with a cream-skimmer, a long-handled ladle full of holes to allow the skim milk to run back into the pan. Cream made from separated milk was never judged to be as good, either in texture or flavour, as cream made from whole raw milk and we still make cream in the old-fashioned way for our own use.

The women of the household used to be responsible for the poultry, and the egg-money was considered to be the wife's own personal pocket-money to be disposed of as she chose. If she were a really good poultrywoman she could be financially indpendent and never have to ask for anything.

Raising poultry was then a matter of dealing with broody hens, each in her own hen-coop, who might, with luck, rear a dozen or so chicks at a time. A hen known to be a good sitter and a good mother — for some clumsy hens trod unmercifully on their newly hatched babies — would be preserved to a ripe old age provided that she lay a few eggs each spring. The wooden hen-coops, made by one of the village carpenters, had a solid front panel which must be removed every morning, revealing the mother-hen confined behind wooden bars that were spaced to allow the chicks to run out into a covered run. The occupants of each coop must be fed and watered several times daily and then carefully shut up at night. Male chicks were sometimes caponised but in any case were grown on for the table, and the pullets were reared as future layers. Most farms still had the ancient stone and slate fowl-house with tiers of wooden perches and a few simple boxes in which the hens were supposed to lay their eggs. Usually the hens had other ideas and when sharp-eyed children found a well-hidden nest of fresh eggs, or better still a nest with a boody hen sitting firmly on her clutch, they would rush to the house to claim a reward. Guinea fowl and bantams usually nested in trees. Bantam hens would lead out a brood of tiny speckled babies from some secret nest and guard them against all comers, foxes, hawks, rats and other enemies. Geese and ducks had to be watched by day and carefully shut up at night. As the light summer evenings lengthened the wretched ducks would still be disporting themselves on the farm pond while a weary maidservant stood impotently at the water's edge, yawning, and simply waiting to shut them up, take her candle, and go to bed.

Very often the women had charge of the fattening pigs, which were either Long White Lop-eared or Large Blacks, two favourite local breeds. Lop-eared pigs were preferred because, as their ears covered their eyes, they were considered to be more docile than prick-eared pigs. The piggeries were cleverly built in a long row, with one side facing the farmyard and the other an orchard or field. The main sty doors opened on to the orchard, but on the yard side there were small doors part-way up the wall, inside which were granite feeding troughs. When these doors were opened the pig-swill could be tipped straight down into the trough. The pig immediately got busy. There was thus no danger of being knocked down by a huge fattening sow, or of having one's bucket sent flying.

Orphan lambs were naturally handed over to the women, although shepherding was normally a man's job, for the local breed of Devon Longwools was a heavy one. Rearing orphan lambs was yet another time-consuming job, especially if there were several of them. Each pathetic little creature presented a human challenge, which had nothing to do with its economic value, and one to which even the children responded.

To return to the buildings ranged around the farmyard: there would be shippons for twenty to forty beasts all with headwalks and hay-lofts overhead, and calves houses with from four to six pens. In those days multiple suckling was more common than pail feeding with whole milk. There were yearling houses, a bull's house with enclosure, a waggon linhay, an implement house and a trap house. Several farms also had a milling chamber which contained a threshing machine driven by a water-wheel. All had big upper-storey barns for storing hay, grain and wool. As yet, in 1919, there was only one building in the whole parish called 'A Garage' or a Trap-house. This shadow of things to come was at Trenance, so passed swiftly into the ownership of the Cornwall County Council.

43

*The Clitsome family of Parson's Pool. Mr Clitsome was part-time gardener at the Vicarage and also a smallholder. His cottage is small but the family appear well-dressed and prosperous.*

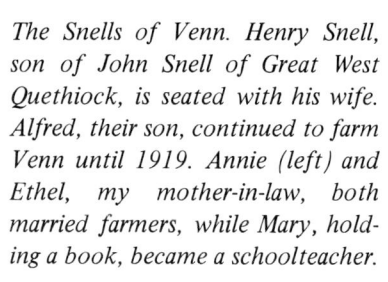

*The Snells of Venn. Henry Snell, son of John Snell of Great West Quethiock, is seated with his wife. Alfred, their son, continued to farm Venn until 1919. Annie (left) and Ethel, my mother-in-law, both married farmers, while Mary, holding a book, became a schoolteacher.*

To give an example of the stock that one of Quethiock's larger farms carried, and for which all these farm buildings were needed, Trehunsey, of 304 acres, had stabling for ten, shippons around the farmyard for thirty-seven, and a nine-sty piggery, as well as yearling houses, calf-houses, and so on. The fat bullocks and stores were here housed in open-fronted linhays in the fields. It will be noted, compared with later years, how small the scale of operations seems to be. Nevertheless it must be borne in mind that inputs were a mere fraction of those that became common in later years. The number of pigs kept was limited by the amount of home-grown barley, and the skim milk available. The number of cows was not only limited by the keep available but also by the labour of hand-milking and the even more laborious task of butter-making. The number of fattening bullocks was limited by the grass available — in those days they fattened on grass, not grain, and were often kept for three years — and also on the hay and roots available for them in winter. From five to fifteen acres of oats must be grown on every farm for the horses, who also had first claim on the best hay because dusty hay would make them cough. Unlike tractors, they were self-replacing but the replacements also had to be fed.

At this point I would like to pause for a moment: I began by saying that life on a farm meant mud, darkness, and much inconvenience. I have gone on to describe some of the tasks that confronted every farm worker, many of them inescapable daily tasks. Yet I have asserted that men and women sang as they went about their daily work, and have asked why. One answer might well be that so many of them sincerely loved their horses, and not only because they were good, well-matched teams who were essential for the working of the farm. No, it was much more than that. The favourite horses, like the favourite dogs, were companions who were talked to, coaxed, sworn at, and sung to, but the most important fact was that many of them were truly loved, so that grooming them became a pleasure rather than a tedious chore. Many a tough farmer used to stay up all night with an ailing horse rather than leave it to one of his men. Today, many retired farmers still have treasured photographs of prize-winning teams proudly displayed on living-room walls, and sometimes of delightful groups of mares with their foals. Tractors, of course, are born adult. I suppose that they are admired by their owners, perhaps even envied by others with older models, but rarely, I imagine, loved. A man would certainly look a fool singing away to a tractor in his implement shed!

Trehunsey employed six men and two chaps, as well as one or two maidservants, at the beginning of the century. There were six farm cottages for the workmen, four of them situated in the village of Quethiock, one in the village of St Ive, and one at Trehunsey itself. Wives of the workmen were accustomed to helping in the farmhouse at busy times, such as for spring-cleaning, or after a pig had been killed for the house, and also outdoors for hay and corn harvesting and for dropping and picking potatoes. All the children helped at these times. So did all the neighbours who converged upon the harvestfields from all directions, often bringing with them their own horses and waggons. No neighbouring farmer was ever paid for his assistance, except by returned labour. Careful note was always kept by each farmer of labour 'owed' and in due course the debt was always honoured. In my book 'Worm in the Wheat' I have described the unpaid neighbourly help given on a threshing day. It was also freely given at harvest time. Perhaps, in this neighbourly helpfulness, in meaningful communal work, with masters and men not only working together but also sharing meals at the same common table, one may find yet another reason why, in spite of all the odds, men were happy. Every farmer was expected to be a good neighbour, so almost all were.

Hay harvest is a good example of how farmers helped one another. This was always an anxious time in a high-rainfall area such as Quethiock. Before the advent of the tractor hay-harvest began with the cutting of the grass with a mowing-machine drawn by a pair of horses. There were no mechanical turners then, so every available pair of hands helped to turn the hay with pikes and forks. When it was half-dry it was usually stacked into pooks in order to keep out any possible rain while drying continued. Then on the first really settled sunny day all the pooks would be scattered abroad and special attention given to any wet 'locks', that is, lumps of still-green grass. When all was judged fit the single-horse hay-rake would arrive on the field and tip the hay into long regular rows called dram-rows. Finally the waggons would come to load it up, usually with two men to 'make' the load and four others to 'pitch-up'. Sometimes the hay-rick might be made in a corner of the same field, at others the hay might be carted back to the mowhay adjacent to the farmyard. Making the rick was always considered to be a very skilled job, quite apart from the thatching with reed (wheat straw) which came later. A well-made, and well-thatched, row of ricks in his mowhay must have given tremendous satisfaction to every farmer, not only because they were an insurance against winter scarcity, but because they were handsome to look at, splendid evidence of his, and his workmen's skill.

Quantities of cider were consumed on these thirsty occasions except on the strictly teetotal farms where lashings of hot and cold tea were substituted. At the end of each harvest day the Missis always provided a substantial tea or supper for the helpers, after which they must all disperse to their own farms, where all their evening tasks were still awaiting them. Nevertheless, tired as they must have been, they always sang as they shouldered their hay-forks and trudged homeward along the narrow lanes. They usually sang well-known hymns such as "Jesu, lover of my soul", and in beautiful harmony. What is more, they sang just as sweetly on cold tea as on cider.

At this time every Quethiock farm had its own large orchard, chiefly of cider-apple trees, and often its own cider-press, but many used the Squire's communal pound-house in the village, built by the roadside for the convenience of his tenants. To this small thatched building farmers could bring their sacks of ripe cider-apples to be squeezed into 'cheese' between two great granite stones. The lower stone had a deep groove all around it, and a lip, over which the unfermented apple juice dripped into a wooden barrel. This process often took more than one day. The school-house was not far from the pound-house and the school-children took turns in operating the two handles that squeezed the cheese. They also brought with them long straws so that they could suck up apple-juice from the barrel, and if there were sacks of apples around, to return to school with bulging pockets. The communal pound-house has been dismantled long since, and even the cider-orchards have vanished.

There were many other occasions throughout the farming year when neighbourly help was freely given, for instance at sheep-shearing and dipping times, and, most important of all, at the time of corn harvest.

Now, by contrast, each farm is its own separate business except insofar as agricultural contractors are called in, on a strictly cash basis, to undertake specialist jobs. The farmer now relies, not on his neighbours, but upon powerful machinery. As he operates his power-driven implements from his lonely seat in the tractor cab he obviously cannot sing because of the rattle; perhaps he can reflect ruefully upon the size of the overdraft which all this expensive and sophisticated equipment has made inevitable. Oddly enough, although his farming pace is no longer that of a pair of plodding horses but of fast powerful machines, today's farmer seems to have less real leisure than his late-Victorian counterpart. Of course his work-force is now down to a bare minimum, and uncomfortably beyond it in some cases. This may explain the necessity for Sunday cultivations, and the fact that so few farmers can now find time to join in parish activities, even for attendance at church or chapel. Sometimes one wonders whether they have really benefited from the abolition of so many of the traditional, skilled tasks. This question of being able to exercise one's own personal skill and judgement is, I suggest, of first importance if men and women are to be happy and contented with their work. I have already described some of the skilled jobs undertaken by farm women, the butter-making and the baking with a cloam oven. Most Quethiock women made all their own and their children's clothes, also their household linen, including delightful patchwork quilts and intricate hand-crocheted bedspreads. How did they ever find the time? I suspect that it was yet another example of 'Waste not. Want not.' They never wasted potato peelings. They never wasted time.

I should now like to describe two skilled jobs undertaken by the men of the farm, the first a very humble, but essential one which has, I think, rarely been described; the second, one with which everyone is familiar. I shall first describe the annual making of the faggots needed as fuel for the cloam oven, from 400 to 1,000 in number according to the fuel supply in hand and the amount of baking likely to be done. Every farm kept a two-year fuel supply in hand. After the autumn ploughing of ley fields their hedges would be cut and rigged-out in the field. Good straight poles would be set aside for fencing, sycamore and ash being good quick growers for this purpose. Other poles would be brought home and neatly stacked, to be sawn into logs later. The faggots were made from small sticks cut from the main wood into 2½ foot lengths and then bound into bundles, some 3 feet in diameter, by flexible withy or nuttall (hazel) some 5 feet long, twisted and tied with a loop. When enough faggots had been made they would be carted back to the farm and made into a rick as close to the back door of the house as possible. It was a matter of pride to construct the rick as neatly as possible, and finally it was thatched to keep the faggots dry. Even the sawn logs were stacked so meticulously that not one single log stood out an inch from his fellows. Wood had to be used in proper rotation for after being cut for about two years many woods go 'sleepy' and lose weight.

Ploughing Quethiock's oddly-shaped and irregularly sloping fields was a challenging task that needed both skill and judgement. As a field was not ploughed in the same direction twice, the ploughman first of all had to bear in mind how the job had been done previously. Then he would choose one of the longer hedges and begin ploughing about five yards distant from it. This five yard furrow-end, or foreland, was necessary for turning the horses and was ploughed last of all. Two horses with a single-furrow plough used to take about a week to plough a five-acre field. Now this is a five-hour job with a tractor! Skill was needed to judge the depth of the plough, usually five to seven inches, the width of the furrow, approximately ten inches, and, most important of all, the pitch, in order to get the furrow at the correct angle. It was essential that it should not fall too flat and so be unable to shed rain, of which Quethiock had plenty. Good ploughmen and their teams worked very steadily and slowly so that the ream holding the furrow would not break as it turned over. A well-ploughed field was always, as it still is, a source of great pride and satisfaction to the ploughman. All cultivations were strictly bound by the Coryton leases, which are of special interest to conservationists and organic farmers. An example will be given in full presently.

In these modern days of bureaucratic paper-work and form-filling, of the buying and selling of other people's products, and of factory assembly lines, the past delights and satisfactions of pure craftsmanship in one's normal daily work is too often forgotten. Farm pay was rotten, but the joy of doing a job as well as possible, was real. The challenge of making neat and uniform faggots of wood, of constructing a comely dry-stone wall, of thatching a rick, or of undertaking hundreds of other farm jobs called for skills that involved co-ordination of hands, eyes, and personal judgement. The craftsman had to understand the qualities of many different natural materials. He took his time about whatever he was doing in order to make as perfect a job of it as possible. One of the great differences between the majority of today's workers, and those of the past, lies in this question of perfection. All true craftsmen aim at perfection, but when the chief aim is high profit, or high wages, painstaking craftsmanship is ruled out. However, before the first world war the men and women of Quethiock aimed at perfection in a multitude of humble tasks, some of which I have described. They had a simple and good relationship with the natural world about them, including the farm stock, and were in a fundamentally harmonious relationship with one another.

An important reason that made for personal happiness in those days was the robust good health of so many people, not the modern, negative type of health that involves a great deal of pill-taking and frequent visits to the doctor for reassurance, but absolute, positive good health. Earlier in the nineteenth century Quethiock had had its tragic toll of untimely deaths, particularly of new-born infants and sometimes of whole families of young children, presumably from diphtheria, scarlet fever, and other infectious diseases. But by the 1880's it had become rare for a child to die and the deaths registered were increasingly those of old people, sometimes very old indeed. At the end of this section is a table showing the ages of the children of Joseph and Fanny Wenmoth of Goodmerry, a typical hard-working farm family who were brought up on a farm such as I have described, and whose longevity is by no means unusual. It greatly interested me to discover that so many old Quethiock folk have remained mentally alert as well as physically active, extremely independent and still enjoying life.

Mrs John Udy Andrews at the garden gate of Furslow, one of Quethiock's oldest farmhouses. Her son, George, married Flora Wenmoth.

John Snell of Great West Quethiock, aged 90, and still able to go about his fields and take an interest in the work of his holding. One of his daughters stands by the garden gate. This photograph was taken by the Rev. Augustus Wix in 1900. John Snell was born in 1809, son of George Snell, farmer, and when he was 29 he married Sarah Udy, daughter of John Udy, farmer. He died when he was 92. When he was born Napoleon was still the Emperor of France and Waterloo had yet to come.

One reason for their tough constitutions may well be that they ate, as growing children and young adults, good, really fresh, and completely unadulterated food. When they were young milk came straight from the cow and the daily junkets were made from it while it was still warm. Bread was home-baked from whole wheat ground in the parish. Eggs were free-range and laid that day. The fruit and vegetables eaten at dinner had probably been still sunning themselves in the kitchen garden half-an-hour before. As sugar was one of the items that must be bought it was used sparingly, and a good thing too. Meals were normally eaten in a very leisurely manner. Daily hard exercise in the fresh air, especially the many miles of walking, gave everyone a healthy appetite while the relaxed pace of life, the absence of worry and tension, no doubt helped digestion.

I believe the farmers of Quethiock had yet another reason for happiness. They knew that they were farming as they should, and that subject to the sensible conditions of their leases they were their own masters, who would stand or fall by their own decisions. They accepted the limitations of their leases because they understood why, with the exception of dairy products and eggs, nothing ought to go off their farms unless it walked off. They did not sell precious fertility and then try and replace it with chemicals, nor did they have to cope with the obscure rulings of the E.E.C., nor try to understand the great swindle of the Green Pound. At breakfast-time they could relax. There was no stream of ghastly news from newspaper or radio to remind them that their native land was now dependent upon charity. There were only weekly papers and no radio. Britain did not depend upon charity but upon work, and they knew it. Out in the yard the farmers would hear the familiar sounds of their men going about their morning tasks, skilled men who knew their jobs and needed no supervision. There was no degrading factory-farming, the farmer, his wife, and all the farm staff could be proud of their stock. So, even though holidays were almost unheard of, and wages and profits low, there was contentment of mind. Is it not a fine thing to be master, within reasonable limits, of one's own destiny?

I will now end this section about Quethiock's larger farms and their farmers with four tables. The first gives the ages, to 1977, of the Wenmoth family of Goodmerry. The second records two pages from Richard Wenmoth's account book, his income and expenditure for the month of March, 1914, while he was farming at Hepwell. Thirdly there is a list of the eighteen farms about which I have been writing, with some details. Finally, I have reproduced in full a representative Coryton lease, for Hammett Farm, which may be of special interest to organic farmers, and to conservationists in general.

Ages of Joseph Wenmoth, Farmer, of Good merry, Quethiock, his wife and children

| Parents | Born | Died, Aged | Living, Aged (at April 1977) |
|---|---|---|---|
| Joseph Wenmoth | 1850 | 88 | |
| Flora Wenmoth | 1852 | 78 | |
| *Children* | | | |
| Richard | 1879 | 78 | |
| Flora | 1881 | | 96 |
| Wilfred | 1882 | 81 | |
| James | 1883 | 81 | |
| Kate | 1885 | | 92 |
| Anne | 1888 | | 88 |
| Bessie | 1890 | 83 | |
| Carrie | 1892 | | 84 |

Joseph Wenmoth's three sons all became farmers, and three daughters married farmers.
One, Bessie, remained unmarried.

Income and Expenditure for March 1914, from Richard Wenmoth's Account Book.
He was then farming Hepwell, 133 acres.

### Income

|       |    |                                     | £   | s  | d  |
|-------|----|-------------------------------------|-----|----|----|
| March | 5  | H. Ough for marketing butter        | 1   | 19 | 3  |
| ”     | 9  | Sold 5 Couples at Liskeard          | 16  | 15 | 0  |
|       |    | 2 barren ewes                       | 4   | 17 | 0  |
|       |    | Mr Spear for 42 bushels of wheat    | 16  | 16 | 0  |
|       |    | Mr Spear for 6 qrs of Oats          | 5   | 5  | 0  |
| ”     | 12 | Mother paid for pork                |     | 11 | 8  |
|       |    | Mother paid for rabbits             |     | 8  | 8  |
|       |    | H. Ough for marketing               | 1   | 13 | 11 |
| ”     | 19 | H. Ough for marketing               | 1   | 15 | 11 |
| ”     | 21 | C. Hares ½ bag potatoes             |     | 2  | 3  |
|       |    | T. Hares ½ bag potatoes             |     | 2  | 3  |
| ”     | 26 | H. Ough for marketing               | 1   | 17 | 0  |
| ”     | 17 | Income Tax refunded                 | 6   | 14 | 2  |
|       |    | Game rate refunded                  |     | 14 | 2  |
| ”     | 27 | Mr Braund for Wool                  | 38  | 15 | 10 |
|       |    | Mr Panter for 2 Fat Bullocks        | 38  | 5  | 0  |
| ”     | 30 | F. Riddle ½ bag potatoes            |     | 2  | 3  |
| ”     | 31 | R. Barrett had a pig                | 1   | 11 | 0  |
|       |    | TOTAL                               | £138| ·6 | 4  |

### Expenditure

|       |    |                                          | £   | s  | d  |
|-------|----|------------------------------------------|-----|----|----|
| March | 6  | Paid S. Smith for Molecatching           |     | 2  | 10 |
|       |    | Mr Harris Groceries                      |     | 1  | 3  |
|       |    | Butcher                                  |     | 3  | 7  |
|       |    | Insurance Stamps                         |     | 7  | 0  |
|       |    | Pd Mr Conway for gravel                  |     | 4  | 0  |
| ”     | 9  | Paid Mr Morcom (Agricultural Merchant)   | 3   | 11 | 0  |
|       |    | Paid Mr Faul (Ironmonger)                |     | 8  | 6  |
|       |    | Paid Robin's for Breeches                |     | 12 | 6  |
| ”     | 10 | Paid Butcher                             |     | 4  | 10 |
|       |    | Spent at Liskeard                        | 2   | 5  | 0  |
| ”     | 17 | Paid Rent ½ year                         | 76  | 10 | 0  |
|       |    | Paid S. Hawken's Bill (Carpenter)        | 5   | 13 | 0  |
|       |    | Paid Butcher                             |     | 6  | 9  |
| ”     | 28 | Paid Butcher                             |     | 1  | 3  |
|       |    | *Paid Albert (workman)                   | 1   | 12 | 0  |
|       |    | *Paid Johnny (chap)                      |     | 5  | 0  |
|       |    | Bindertwine from Mr Snell                | 1   | 14 | 0  |
|       |    | TOTAL                                    | £94 | 2  | 6  |

\* 1st entry. Paid fortnightly, plus food.

*A smart turnout. Ann Snell, of Trenance, with Tom Thumb.*

*A pet lamb that had grown too big for comfort. Mrs Ann Snell, of Trenance tries—unsuccessfully—to slip out of her garden unobserved.*

## LAND USE

Quethiock's 18 farms of over 100 acres, plus Holwood, 458 acres.

1. **Trenance**
   153 acres   Rent £270 p.a.   2 cottages at Blunts.
   Arable 96a 3r,   Pasture 52a 2r,   Orchard 2 acres.
   Water wheel to drive Threshing Machine and Mill.
   Timber valued at £10.   Dairy and Corn Farm.

2. **Luccombe**
   106 acres   Rent £137 p.a.   3 cottages, two of them at Blunts.
   Arable 58a 1r,   Pasture 40a 2r,   Orchard & Woods 5 acres.
   Timber valued at £60.   Dairy, Sheep and Corn Farm.

3. **Penpoll**
   125 acres   Rent £199 p.a.
   Arable 86a 3r,   Pasture 35a 1r,   Orchard 1a 1r.
   Timber valued at £9.   Dairy & Corn Farm.

4. **Tilland**
   119 acres   Rent £137 p.a.   3 cottages at Blunts.
   Arable 38a 1r,   Pasture 73a 1r,   Orchard & Woods 5 acres.
   Timber valued at £140.   Corn, Sheep & Dairy Farm.
   Water Wheel to drive Threshing Machine.

5. **Haye**
   172 acres   Rent £230 p.a.   1 cottage at Trehunist.
   Arable 122 acres,   Pasture 43a 3r,   Orchard 4 acres.
   Timber valued at £26.   Dairy, Sheep & Corn Farm.

6. **Trebrown**
   149 acres   Rent £218 p.a.   1 cottage.
   Arable 66a 2r. Pasture 67a 2r, Orchard & Woods 12 acres.
   Timber valued at £360.   Dairy, Sheep & Corn Farm.

7. **Goodmerry**
   167 acres   Rent £125 p.a.   1 cottage at Trewood.
   Arable 107 acres,   Pasture 33a 3r,   Orchard & Woods 18a 2r.
   Timber valued at £920.   Dairy, Sheep & Corn Farm.

8. **Leigh**
   242 acres   Rent £188 p.a.   1 cottage.
   Arable 110a 2r,   Pasture 67a 2r,   Orchard & Woods 54 acres.
   Timber valued at £928.   Corn, Sheep & Dairy Farm.
   (Total acreage includes 7 acres of marsh.)

9. **Furslow**
   225 acres   Rental £162 p.a.
   Arable 138 acres,   Pasture 76a 1r,   Orchards & Woods 7a 1r.
   Timber valued at £80.   Corn & Rearing Farm.
   (Pasture includes 45 acres of downland.)

10. **Dannett**
    147 acres   Rent £110 p.a.
    Arable 90a 2r,   Pasture 24a 3r,   Orchards & Woods 29a 1r.
    Timber and Coppice valued at £540.   Corn & Sheep Farm.
    (Apple Press and Mill.)

11 **Hammett**
 174 acres   Rent £165 p.a.   1 cottage.
 Arable 108 acres,   Pasture 44a 2r,   Orchard & Woods 8a 3r.
 Timber & Coppice valued at £110.   Dairy, Sheep & Corn Farm.
 (Total acreage includes 8 acres of marsh.)
 Water Wheel to drive Threshing Machine and Mill.

12 **Trecorme**
 192 acres   Rent £240 p.a.   1 cottage.
 Arable 137a 2r,   Pasture 39a 2r,   Orchards & Woods 5 acres.
 Timber valued at £50.   Corn, Sheep & Dairy Farm.
 (Total acreage includes 8 acres of marsh, Mill Pond, and Leat to Trecorme Mill.)

13 **Trehunist East**
 108 acres   Rent £175 p.a.   1 cottage.
 Arable 85a 3r,   Pasture 19a 1r,   Orchard 2a 2r.
 Timber valued at £6.   Corn, Sheep and Dairy Farm.

14 **Trehunist West**
 166 acres   Rent 265 p.a.   2 cottages.
 Arable 117a 1r,   Pasture 44a 2r,   Orchard & Wood 2a 2r.
 Timber valued at £8.   Corn, Sheep & Dairy Farm.

15 **East Quethiock**
 143 acres   Rent £150 p.a.   2 cottages in Village.
 Arable 118a 1r,   Pasture 19 acres,   Orchard & Wood 4a 1r.
 Timber valued at £125.   Corn, Sheep & Dairy Farm.

16 **Hepwell**
 133 acres   Rent £154 p.a.   1 cottage.
 Arable 95 acres,   Pasture 25 acres,   Woods 10 acres.
 Timber valued at £140.   Corn, Sheep & Dairy.

17 **Treweese**
 140 acres   Rent £168 p.a.   3 cottages in village.
 Arable 99 acres,   Pasture 31a 1r,   Orchard & Woods 7 acres.
 Timber valued at £195.   Corn, Sheep & Dairy Farm.
 (Hepwell Mill House added to this farm.)

18 **Trehunsey**
 304 acres   Rent £226 p.a.   6 cottages, 4 in Quethiock village, 1 on farm, 1 St Ive
 Arable 232a 3r,   Pasture 36a 2r,   Orchard & Woods 38a 3r.
 Timber valued at £785.   Dairy, Sheep & Corn Farm.
 Water wheel for threshing and reed combing.
 (Formerly this farm had a water-mill on the R. Tiddy.)

*Note*

The total acreage of these 18 farms includes the figures for houses, garden plots, yards and buildings, also roads and small ponds. Therefore in all cases it will be slightly higher than the total acreage for arable, pasture, orchards and woods combined, as houses, etc., are excluded.

**Holwood**
458 acres   Rent £525 p.a.   6 cottages on Estate.
Arable 105a 2r,   Pasture 281a 3r,   Woods & Orchard 55a 1r.
Agricultural, Residential and Sporting Estate, with a mile frontage to R. Lynher affording Good Fishing. Well-wooded Coverts, affording Excellent Shooting.
Timber valued at £1,050.
The Lands were, until recently, for many years in the occupation of W. Coryton, Esq., and are in a high state of cultivation.

Lease dated March 25th 1871 for Hammett Farm, Quethiock,
(excepting Timber and Sporting Rights)

Lease for 7 or 14 years Yearly rent £100 (151 acres)

(I)     Augustus Coryton, Esq.

(II)    Wm Cannon, Hammett, Quethiock, Yeoman.

Hammett Farm in Quethiock containing 151a .2r 20p. occ. (II). Full reservations including cottages and cottage gardens and hunting etc., also water flowing through the farm towards Trecorme Mills and the pond on the farm. (II) could have use of water for driving machinery and for irrigation whenever landlord or agent thought it could be used without detriment to the working of Trecorme Mill. Term ending at 7 years to have 12 months notice by either party. (II) to pay taxes including land tax and tithe rent charge. (II) to repair everything except main timbers, main walls and slated roofs, landlord providing timber for (II) to fetch, (II) to fetch also all materials required for landlord's repairs. Landlord to pay cost of thatching, tenant supplying reeds, spears and cord for the same.

Tenant to look after orchards, fence and secure trees and keep fully planted. Orchards not to be stocked except with sheep and pigs. (II) to cleanse all ditches and water-courses. Except for hedges annually clipped not to cut any wood from the hedges unless same be of six years growth or upwards, and then only from hedges bounding the fields in wheat tillage and between the months of November and March. No wood to be cut in last year of the term. Not more than one-sixth of land scheduled as arable, which has been sown with grass seeds and kept in pasture not less than three years previously, to be broken up for wheat or grain crops. Turnips or other green crops to be properly cleansed and cultivated and manured with not less than 20 cartloads of good rotten farm-dung or 2½ qrs of genuine bone dust per acre. For barley or oats not less than 10 pounds of clover and ten pounds of eaver seeds per acre to be sown therewith.

Landlord to supply grass seeds in the last year of the tenancy or to pay cost to tenant who is to sow and harrow in the seeds. Grass seeds to be cut for hay or grazed at the option of the tenant but not to be cut more than once. Pasture to be grazed.

(II) could take a crop of barley or oats immediately following the wheat crops, but if barley or oat crop taken it is to be manured (or the wheat crop immediately preceding) with 50 bushels of lime per acre.

(II) not to break up in any one year more than one-seventh of the acreable extent of arable land and shall extend the course to seven years instead of six. Provided that the acreable proportion under turnips or other green crop be not lessened in any year by such alteration in the rotation of cropping. No more than three acres of potatoes to be grown in any one year. Straw and dung to be consumed on the premises. Tenant could sell hay and wheat reed. (II) not to break up fields scheduled as meadow or pasture and not to cut land (except fields scheduled as 'Water Meadow') for hay, unless manured with not less than 20 cartloads of good rotten dung per acre. (II) to allow landlord or incoming tenant into land in course to break for wheat on 1 July. One-fifth of such Arish or Stubble ground as comes in course for Turnips or other Green Crop the following year, on and after the first day of September to till Vetches or other crop for soiling. And all the Arishes for ploughing the same and any ground on which Potatoes may have grown on and after December 1st. (II) not to stock grass seeds after the first day of November and up to then with sheep and pigs only. (II) to give room for two horses or working cattle etc. to allow landlord or incoming tenant to use the manure. Landlord to allow (II) use of barn and room for two horses and stalls for consuming turnips or other root crops and straw or hay until June 1st after expiration of tenancy.

54

On 24th October 1889 Henry Snell, farmer, aged 38, son of Joseph Snell, farmer of East Quethiock, married Ann Charlton, 29, daughter of Matthew Charlton, farmer of Holwood. Here they are, some years later, with Mary Charlton (left) sister to Ann.

Charlie Jane of Clemasis, Blunts, uncle to Bill Jane and gamekeeper to Squire William, with his friend Jim Hatch (left) farm worker of Dunnerdake, St. Ive.

55

# The Smaller Farms

In this section I shall describe Quethiock's smaller farms and small-holdings as they existed until the summer of 1919. But first, because so many people today have been conditioned into believing that 'bigger is better', and may assume therefore that this section is bound to be of less importance than the last, may I say with all emphasis at my command that nothing, absolutely nothing, could be further from the truth.

These small farms and small-holdings were of major social importance because they provided the essential first rungs of the farming ladder upon which an able and hard-working man, with no assets beyond drive and a good wife, could climb until he became his own master. This farming ladder had existed for many centuries. It was not an easy one to climb but it had always been there. Now it is gone. Today the increasing polarisation between those, on the one hand, who own large acreages and are able to finance large-scale, highly mechanised and highly capitalised farming operations and those, on the other, who actually work in agriculture as hired hands, whether as manual labourers, skilled stockmen, craftsmen or college-trained managers, makes nonsense of any poor man's dream of ever becoming his own boss. The present capital requirements needed to enter farming even on the most modest scale, and even on a subsidised County Council holding, puts any such project quite beyond the reach of any man without access to substantial assets. It is a very great loss, particularly so for those thinking young people who already understand the hard and dangerous times ahead for the over-industrialised countries that are unable to feed themselves. These young people would like to do something practical. A widely-travelled educationalist wrote to me recently: "You may find our experience interesting, in that we see among young people a distinct reversion back to natural ways and methods."

At the end of this section I shall recall some of an exceptionally interesting life story, that of a retired farmer who was born in 1881, which illustrates how a man born into very humble circumstances could formerly climb the ladder from workman to master.

This mobility, this constant spur to personal endeavour, was possible because of two essential factors. First, the farming structure of the parish of Quethiock, as of the surrounding parishes that formed part of the Coryton estate, was extraordinarily flexible, that is to say, there was a great variety of size of farms and small-holdings to rent, and, as so many formed part of the one great estate, moving up, or down, as in retirement, was relatively easy. A man could not buy his way into these farms. He had to be known for his farming ability and his personal integrity, although naturally he needed to be able to command the means to stock and cultivate his farm in the accepted manner.

While this great variety of farm size was one important part of the ladder the other, which I suggest was equally important, was the fact that the pay-structure of the Quethiock agricultural worker was as flexible and as varied as the size of the farms. Most working men in the parish, even those who considered themselves as primarily wage-earners in the employ of one farmer, also owned some stock, certainly the ubiquitous pig, probably some poultry and often a cow. Some villagers rented a little land and then perhaps reared a bullock or two. Other men specialised in a particular craft, such as rick-thatching, and hedge-building, or excelled at killing and dressing pigs. This important combination of wage-work with the extra rewards for a man's own endeavours, or perhaps it would be more correct to say, a family's own endeavours, for the women and children played an important part in all this, meant that there was a genuine road to advancement, with the attainable goal of eventual independence.

In the parish of Quethiock there were ten farms of less than 100 acres, although one of them is on the parish border and the farmhouse is in St Ive, and sixteen small-holdings ranging from nineteen acres down to one. Most of the small-holdings were farmed by men with other principal occupations, as I shall explain presently. Naturally, one would not expect the inn-keeper, the wheelwright or the carpenter to be aspirants to larger holdings, any more than was their Vicar, busily farming his 47 acres of vicarial glebe. Nevertheless many tenants of these little holdings were hoping to move on to a bigger place one day. Meanwhile all of them were producing much of their own food and therefore, because of their minimal claims upon others, had already achieved a definite measure of independence. Even a man with only an acre, or a cottager with none, could, if he so desired, rent a garden plot or a field from a neighbouring farmer. For example the Sale Brochure shows that Mr Alfred Harris, the village shop-keeper, rented 7 acres from Mr John Wills of Trehunsey. These acres consisted of a garden plot, four small pasture fields and one arable field of 2½ acres. Two cottagers, members of the Riddle family, who were all great gardeners, were at the same time renting garden plots on Little West Quethiock Farm, one plot was let to Mr George Riddle at 2s 6d per annum, and the other to Mr F Riddle at 5s 0d per annum. In addition there was plenty of free grazing for small-holders and cottagers stock on the road verges and the hedges. Land was freely available, rents were cheap, and neighbours were obliging.

Here are some particulars of the ten farms of under 100 acres:—

|   | Name | Acreage | Type | Rent (excluding sporting rights) | Sale Price |
|---|---|---|---|---|---|
| 1 | Venn | 97 | Corn, Sheep & Dairy | £117 | £3,550 |
| 2 | Tilland Mill | 87 | Corn & Dairy | £100 | £1,750 |
| 3 | Coombe | 82 | Corn, Sheep & Dairy | £95 | £1,800 |
| 4 | Great West Quethiock | 66 | Dairy, Sheep & Corn | £104 | £2,100 |
| 5 | Great Ley | 52 | Dairy | £75 | £1,850 |
| 6 | Singmoor | 41 | Mixed | £60 | £1,175 |
| 7 | Trehurst | 40 | Dairy | £100 | £2,250 |
| 8 | Venn Hill | 38 | Corn & Sheep | £48 | £1,020 |
| 9 | Gooseford | 37 | Corn & Stock | £29 | £660 |
| 10 | Little West Quethiock | 28 | Dairy & Corn | £56 | £1,950 |

My choice of 100 acres as the dividing line between the larger and the smaller farms is a quite arbitrary one. The largest of the 'small' farms, Venn, was clearly not very different from its slightly bigger neighbours. Like them, it was described as a 'Corn, Sheep & Dairy Farm'. The substantial farmhouse contained four bedrooms and, that status symbol, a drawing-room. The farm buildings were similar to those found on neighbouring farms with a slightly larger acreage. Tilland Mill, with 87 acres, not only had a farmhouse with five bedrooms but was the only house in the parish, apart from Holwood, to boast a modern water-closet, albeit this was only 'close to the house' not in it, as at Holwood. Great West Quethiock farmhouse had five bedrooms and a drawing-room, also a cottage in the village for a farm worker. Nevertheless my choice of 100 acres as the dividing line would seem to be fair enough. Thereafter, as the farm acreages become progressively smaller there is no further mention of drawing-rooms, no second staircase, no farm workers' cottages. These smaller farms were essentially family farms, usually dairy farms which relied heavily upon family labour. It was quite usual for smaller farmers to work occasionally for larger men at busy times, either as paid day-labourers or on a reciprocal basis, while the women customarily carried on the routine work at home.

Undoubtedly some of these women worked too hard, but equally undoubtedly, because they were so absolutely essential to the farm economy and were often financially independent through their own 'butter and egg money', they were accorded a status, and commanded a respect, that few woman in the cities could hope to achieve. These farm women took their authority within the home completely for granted. Because in those days the homestead was the working centre of the farm so their influence extended much further afield, and most of them determined the farm's economic strategy equally with their husbands. There was no aggressiveness about all this. It was the natural outcome of economic inter-dependence within the family unit and of the women's vital contribution to it. Nevertheless it was the custom — in the west-country it still is — for the men to do the talking in public!

I will now give some details of the farmhouses and buildings on two of these smaller farms. It will be seen that there was no specialisation, these small units aimed to be as self-contained and self-sufficient as the larger ones. Singmoor, a mixed farm of 41 acres, had a small modern farmhouse quite unlike the rambling, picturesque older ones with their many-paned windows and their medley of chimneys. Singmoor farmhouse was exactly the functional house that children draw, three sash windows upstairs, two down, with the front door in the middle and a matching chimney at each gable-end. The house contained four bedrooms, two sitting-rooms, a kitchen with an open fireplace, a pantry and a dairy. Outside, in the farmyard, was the essential pump-house, built, like the house and all the other permanent farm buildings, of stone and slate. These comprised a barn, a three-stall stable, two calves houses, a shippon for fourteen, a yearling house with a head-walk, and a root-house with a loft. There were, needless to say, piggeries, two in number with two sties to each. Recently a 2-bay iron cart-shed and implement linhay had been erected. Also the tenant had built himself a wood-and-iron fowl house and a wood-shed against one side of the house. Singmoor had 18 acres of pasture, all in little fields of two acres or less, and 22 acres of arable land. With the sole exception of one field of 8 acres, even the arable fields were equally small, of 2 acres or less. The farm had no orchard, or at anyrate none worth mentioning, and the timber valuation was only £6.

Another small farm of 38 acres, described as a 'Corn & Sheep' farm was Venn Hill, with a stone and slated farmhouse containing five bedrooms, a parlour, a kitchen with a kitchen range, a back kitchen with a furnace and boiler, plus the dairy and pumphouse. The farm buildings at Venn Hill were again substantially built of stone and slate and comprised a 3-stall stable with a loft over, a shippon for eight, a calving pen, a root-house, another shippon for five, a calves' house, a waggon linhay and a 3-sty piggery. Very unusually a coalhouse is also mentioned, unusual because at the time most of the able-bodied people of the parish cut and stacked their own wood and furze. Even the children, as autumn approached, were sent out with old prams and baskets to gather firewood, and told to note where the ripening cob-nuts were thickest. On summer walks the villagers would usually return home with a small bundle of dry sticks. Wood was there for the taking while coal must be bought. Venn Hill had but 7 acres of pasture land, divided into four small fields, and 31 acres of arable land. This was divided into nine enclosures, averaging about three acres per enclosure. There was no mention of any orchard, nor was any figure given for timber valuation.

The people who lived on these smaller farms had a life-style hardly distinguishable from that of their neighbours with larger acreages to whom in many cases they were closely connected by birth or marriage. The women worked somewhat harder for they rarely had any paid domestic help, the children too, for when they became old enough to be of use they were expected to undertake serious work, not just jolly jobs at harvest times and the like, but tedious tasks like walking to Callington market every week with a heavy basket of butter and eggs. Farming is always a risk-taking business, and in those days animal diseases such as tuberculosis, red-water and contagious abortion had not yet been brought under control. Contagious abortion in particular was dreaded by all farmers but for the small dairy farmer it could mean disaster. It meant no milk, therefore no butter and cream to sell, and hence the major source of income lost for a year.

*Drawing timber from Digoridge Wood, Goodmerry. This was hard and muddy work for men and horses.*

*Leisurely farming. A quiet lane, a few peaceful cows attended by two men with plenty of time to spare.*

Fortunately family and friends always rallied round. There would be offers of paid work to tide the family over the crisis months. There would be extra gifts of food, and of clothes for the children, indeed the practical realities of extended-family assistance meant that no deserving family would ever be allowed to 'go scat' because of undeserved misfortune, and it was done in such a manner that a man could keep his pride. It helped, naturally, that everyone knew everybody else's business. How could it be otherwise? Quite apart from the intricate web of family connections all the children of the parish, with only one or two exceptions, attended the same village school. Still together, a little older, they joined in all the village fun, the cricket matches, dancing around the blacksmith's maypole, singing in the church or chapel choir, and going on outings to the sea-side at Looe. They competed in the horticultural shows and the ploughing matches; they took part, either as performers or audience, in the penny readings and the more ambitious village concerts. It meant that there could be very little social distinction between the larger and the smaller farmers, except perhaps that the two churchwardens were invariably farmers of substance. On the other hand the Quethiock Wesleyan Methodist Church included among its Trustees, not only five farmers but also Mr Alfred Harris, the village grocer, his son, Louis Harris, the miller at Trecorme Mill, and Benjamin and Sidney Hawken, carpenters and wheelwrights, of Treweese Cross. Many years were to pass before a woman became a Trustee, but in 1932 Miss Hettie Harris, spinster, daughter of Alfred Harris, was able to carry on the family tradition.

The Small-holdings

|    | Name                  | Acres | Rent (excluding sporting rights) | Occ. of Tenant | Sale Price |
|----|-----------------------|-------|----------------------------------|----------------|------------|
| 1  | The 'Mason's Arms'    | 19    | £45                              | Publican       | £925       |
| 2  | Parson's Park         | 17    | £47.10                           | Retired Farmer | £1,210     |
| 3  | Clapper Bridge        | 15    | £24                              | —              | £400       |
| 4  | Trecorme Mill         | 9     | £27.10                           | Miller         | £520       |
| 5  | Enquire the Way       | 7     | £14                              | Farm Worker    | £250       |
| 6  | Sopers                | 7     | £10                              | Farm Worker    | £210       |
| 7  | Trehunist Smallholding| 7     | £18.10                           | Farm Worker    | £300       |
| 8  | Trebrowngate          | 6     | £21                              | Farm Worker    | £525       |
| 9  | Lower Pounda          | 6     | £14.10                           | Carpenter      | £390       |
| 10 | Higher Pounda         | 3     | £10                              | Blacksmith     | £220       |
| 11 | Treweese Cross        | 3     | £14                              | Wheelwright    | £350       |
| 12 | Broadapark            | 3     | £9                               | Farm Worker    | £170       |
| 13 | Birch Hill            | 3     | £10                              | Mason          | £225       |
| 14 | Quarry Garden         | 1     | £8                               | A Widow        | £200       |
| 15 | Village Stores        | 1     | £25                              | Shopkeeper     | £450       |
| 16 | Parson's Pool         | 1     | £6.10                            | Sawyer         | £170       |

It will be seen that many of the tenants of these small-holdings had another major source of livelihood, which I have given. Therefore in most cases much of the routine work of the holding was undertaken by the wife who milked the cow, or cows, grazed them upon the roadside wastes, fed pigs and poultry, and maintained the flower and fruit garden. Vegetable production, bee-keeping and water-carrying were men's jobs. Nevertheless the small-holders' wives, like the small farmers' wives, were busy from morning till night, for cooking, washing, ironing and cleaning had to be carried out without benefit of labour-saving devices. No wonder that the wife of one small-holder always kept her dark curly hair cut short like a boy's because, as she explained, she simply had no time to fiddle about with it. Her photograph, however, shows that this style suited her merry face to perfection and no doubt she could handle a mirror as sensibly as a pitch-fork.

One of the hardest workers of all must have been Matilda, wife of the inn-keeper Francis Snell, tenant of The Mason's Arms. Not only must she milk cows, feed bullocks, pigs and poultry like most of the other small-holders' wives, but also, later must process tham into roast barons of beef, roast chine of pork, roast chicken, and dozens of great meat pies. The Mason's Arms was famous for its dinners, and especially its Audit Day Dinners, of which more later. No wonder that poor Matilda, who bore six children in ten years, in addition to all these other tasks, is entered in the Parish Register of Burials thus: "Matilda Snell. Mason's Arms. Quethiock. Jan 13th 1896 Aged 36". Family legend has it that she was found, collapsed and dying, up in the milking shed. However, one must not judge her husband too harshly. Francis Neal had himself been born in The Mason's Arms where his father, Edmund Snell, had been the licensee before him. Edmund had married Loveday Ough in 1829 and they had successfully reared twelve children, of whom Francis Neal was the next to last, the last being my husband's grandmother, Flora Ann. What more natural than that Matilda's husband should take this kind of reproduction-rate for granted?

Trecorme Mill, Quethiock's most important corn mill and the last to cease working (it was only dismantled after the second World War), included nine acres of farmland. The Millhouse was described as substantially built of stone and slate with a powerful over-shot iron and wood water-wheel able to drive two pairs of stones. As well as the five-roomed house with a dairy there was a stone and slated shippon for four, a calving house with headwalk, and loft over, and three calves houses. Naturally, there was a stable, again with a loft overhead, and on the opposite side of the road a 'modern' stone and slated 4-sty piggery. It is still there, with Squire William's red brick trim to prove its modernity eighty years ago. Alas, the sturdy little building has outlasted its pigs. Trecorme Mill was let from 1867 onward to a member of my husband's family, a namesake, an earlier James Wenmoth. The Coryton Estate had put the following advertisement in *The Cornish Times*, dated November 15th, 1867:

> "To be Let by Tender from Xmas next, Dec. 25th, 1867, Trecorme Mills in the Parish of Quethiock consisting of Dwelling house and convenient outbuildings, Millhouse with powerful Water-wheel driving two pairs of Millstones and other necessary machinery, together with about six acres of land."

So James Wenmoth, writing from Treverbyn Mill, St. Neot, sent in his tender as follows:—

> "I hereby will agree to give the sum of £30 per year for the Mill with the ground adjoining called Trecorme Mill in the Parish of Quethiock as advertised in *The Cornish Times* newspaper dated 15 November 1867."
>
> James Wenmoth Son of Jane Wenmoth, Dannett.

The Tender was backed up by a letter from Thomas Parson of Treverbyn Mill, St. Neot, dated 12 Dec. 1867.

> To Mr Snell (Agent)
>
> Dear Sir,
>
> Mr James Wenmoth has been with me for three years and during that time I have found him Upright, Sober and master of his trade as a Miller.
>
> I have great pleasure in bearing testimony to one who has been to me a most satisfactory servant.
>
> I am, Yours respectfully,
>
> Thomas Parson.

*One of the first binders in the parish with John Wills, tenant of 304-acre Trehunsey, in the driver's seat. His men were still nervous of the 'new-fangled machinery' so he, himself, cut other farmers' corn for 2s. 6d. per acre. Reg Wills, his young son, is on horseback and (left) Mr Higman, grandfather of Mrs Welch (see helpers) holds a sheaf of wheat. All the farming photographs, except family groups, were taken between 1895 and 1905.*

*A binder in a barley field at East Quethiock. The farmer, Mr Fred Snell, with his dog, is watching C. Cloake driving it.*

So this Upright, Sober and most satisfactory servant was deservedly rewarded with the tenancy of Trecorme Mill and became his own master. The quitting tenant, the widowed Mrs Jenifer Body who had lived there for over fifty years, now decided to put up the entire contents of the Mill for public auction. The poster which announced that Mr G. Roseveare would sell the farm stock and implements, and also the household furniture, on Tuesday, the 20th December 1867 is a most interesting and informative document, no less than a complete inventory of the typical contents of a small-holding at that time. As in those days most furniture and farming gear was made locally and made to last, the inventory would have been valid for decades.

Parish of Quethiock
To Be Sold at Public Auction at Trecorme Mills
on Friday the 20th December, 1867
the property of Mrs Body, quitting.

**Farm** 1 Prime Dairy Cow, 1 Yearling, 2 Excellent Horses, Plough, Stone Rollers and Frames, Iron Tormentor, Diagonal Harrows, Cart and Wheels, Spring Market Trap and Harness, 5 Granite Pig's Troughs, 1 Large Iron Ditto, Sheep Rack, Empty Casks and Kieves, Grindstone and Frame, Large Flour Hutch, several Wire Sieves, Peck Measure, Sacks and Bags, Beam, Scales & Weights, Large and Small Blocks and Ropes, Horse Harness, Saddle and Bridle and a number of Husbandry Tools, etc.

Also 1 Rick of Hay about 4 tons, 1 Rick of Straw, about 1 Acre of Turnips in convenient Lots, and about ten bags of Prime Potatoes.

**Furniture** Kitchen Table and Form, Shelves and Dressers, Settle, Kitchen Range and Fender, Oven Door and Jambs, Corner Cupboard, Large Meat Trundle, Large Brass Kettle, One Large Boiler, Washing Trays, 2 Bedsteads, Clock and Case, 6 Chairs, a number of Ducks and Fowls and Various other Articles too numerous to mention.

If this humble little sale were taking place now, in 1977, instead of then, in 1867, one can just imagine the press of antique dealers coming from far and wide, jamming the narrow lanes to Trecorme Mill, the excited bidding for the large brass kettle, the settle, the corner cupboard, even the granite pig troughs!

The description of Treweese Cross in the Sale Brochure also illustrates this mixture of craftsmen's trade and small-holding:

There is a Stone-built and Slated House, containing Three Bedrooms, Parlour, Kitchen with Apple Chamber over, Dairy, and Stone and Slated Well House with Well.

Attached to the House is a Stone-built and Slated Carpenter's Shop; Also Two Stone and Slated Piggeries, Wood and Iron Timber Store and Shop, and a Stone-built and felt-roofed Wheelwright's or Blacksmith's Shop: together with Gardens and Pasture Fields, the whole extending to about 3 acres.

In most cases the dwelling houses of the small-holdings were not described in any detail. One exception was Parson's Park, a compact miniature farm much favoured by retiring farmers. Mr George Andrews, husband of the lovely Flora Wenmoth, having but one child, a daughter, and having farmed Leigh's 242 acres for many years, bought it for this purpose at the Sale. The name Parson's Park is an interesting reminder that it was formerly part of the Rectorial Gleve, separated from the Vicarial Glebe in 1337 when the great tithes of Quethiock were appropriated to a Chantry at Haccombe in Devon. Five hundred years later, at the time of the Tithe Apportionment in 1842 the Gross Rent charge payable to the Tithe Owners was:

|  | £ | s | d |
|---|---|---|---|
| To The Vicar of Quethiock | 342 | 9 | 0 |
| To The Rector of Haccombe | 343 | 12 | 0 |
| Total | 686 | 1 | 0 |

and the Rectorial Glebe of West, East and South Parson's Park was then farmed by a John Dingle. Later, it came into the Coryton Estate but retained its old name. Parson's Pool, a much more modest little holding, is named thus for the same historic reason.

Sopers, a holding of seven acres had a cottage of stone, cob and thatch which consisted of a living-room with an open fireplace, a small dairy, and two bedrooms. Adjoining the dwelling-house was a stone, cob and thatched barn, a stone, wood and thatched shippon for three, a meal house and two stone and slated pig's houses. In 1919 Sopers was occupied by a widow, Mrs Olver. One of her sons still lives there. The little cob cottage has tumbled into ruin but Mr Wilfred Olver, a batchelor lives in a caravan by the buildings. He is, primarily, an agricultural worker, but rears a few bullocks on his little piece of land, quite in the old independent tradition. He is certainly the last of his kind. Incidentally there are only two farmers still resident in the parish, both now retired, who were living in the parish in 1919, Mr Henry Kelly, formerly of Trecorme Barton, and now of Trecorme Mill, and Mr Eugene Wenmoth of Great West Quethiock. Although the latter had four sons, not one opted for farming as a career.

The humblest dwelling on my list of small-holdings was probably that known as Part Rombelow, or Broadapark. Its entire description was merely this:

> The freehold stone-built and slated Cottage and Garden, together with the Pasture Field, in area about three acres, and the site of a stable opposite Quethiock Church.

Possibly, even then, the less said about the cottage the better for later it fell into ruin. As to the curious name 'Rombelow', I noted that from 1660 to 1671 the Vicar of the parish had been named Nathaniel Rumbelowe. What more likely than that his horse was once pastured in this field and once occupied the stable formerly on the site 'opposite Quethiock Church'. The Vicarage was one mile distant from the Church. Some two hundred and forty years later the Rev. Augustus Wix, (the Vicar who took so many of the photographs for this book) who apparently used Shank's pony most of the time, calculated that in two and a half years of walking from his Vicarage to the Church and back, three times daily, he had covered 2,737 miles. He mentioned this in his pastoral letter in the Magazine for the Deanery of East Wivelshire in September, 1901. Perhaps it had been a long, hot, dusty summer!

I hope that I have now given an adequate idea of the variety of Quethiock's smaller farms and small-holdings and, above all else, have proved their importance, both as a vital step in the farming ladder and also as units of production which gave the men and women farming them a real measure of independence.

*A load of thatching reed about to be carted from Trehunsey to St. Mellion for Squire William. Mrs Wills, the farmer's wife, her little daughter and the servants are watching the travellers set off. Three of the workforce are members of the same family. Mr Cudmore senior worked for John Wills for over thirty years.*

*Threshing Day at Trehunsey. These were among the busiest days of the farming year, not only for the men working outdoors but also for the women who had to feed them.*

This brings me, finally, to the story of a man who, while opportunities could still be seized by men with little capital, grasped them with both firm, hard-working hands. His entire story confirms the complete contrast between the world into which he was born and that which he could observe around him in his old age. E.H. was born on September 26th, 1881, at Little Larnick, near Looe, East Cornwall, where his father was farming in a small way. Times were hard and money was short, so as well as caring for its stock and crops, the family lost no opportunity to increase its income in other ways. Among E.H.'s earliest memories was driving to Plymouth in a donkey and cart with his father to sell apples and then bring back mackerel to sell around the Pelynt area. When E.H. was about six years old he became dissatisfied with having only one pair of boots. He wanted smart 'best' boots for Sundays, like those worn by the richer children. So his father gave the little lad a patch of ground and some seed potatoes, telling him that he could teel them, keep them weeded and banked, harvest them and sell them. With the money thus earned he would be able to buy himself the desired best Sunday boots. Said the dear old man of 93, who was telling me this tale at his birthday party with many of his family gathered around listening to him, "I can tell you, I was prouder of that first pair of best boots than of any fine footwear I ever bought afterwards."

At Ladyday, 1891, the family moved to a slightly larger farm at Linkinhorne, close to Bodmin Moor. This was just after the Great Blizzard and even at Ladyday snow was still falling. All the cattle had to be walked from Pelynt to Linkinhorne. E.H.'s mother, with a baby in her arms, shared the farm cart with two brood sows over which she had to hold a net. It was bitterly cold and the 20-mile uphill journey, over roads deep in snow, was a nightmare that the boy never forgot. It proved impossible to bring any fodder for the stock but one of their new neighbours willingly lent the family feeding-stuffs until the roads became passable, and so saved them from disaster.

When he was eleven years old E.H. left school and went to work at Clampit Farm. This meant a walk of a mile and a half in order to get to work by 7.0 a.m. Thereafter, with only a short break for mid-day dinner, he worked until 6.0 p.m. Then came the long walk home again. His wage for a 6½ day week — he only had from Sunday lunch-time free so had to walk to Clampit and back every day of the week — was 9d a day plus a free dinner. The dinners must have been good and plentiful for, in spite of all the work and the walking, E.H. grew apace.

The following year, when he was twelve he was hired at Ladyday for twelve months to another local farmer, this time to live in the farmhouse, with a wage of £5 a year. He proved a satisfactory worker, quick to learn and was asked to stay for a second year. He did so, for the farmer's wife was kind and the food was good. He was given a rise of another £1 a year. This employer must have been somewhat careful with his money for E.H. remembered very vividly being taken to Launceston Show by his employer in a pony and trap as a very special treat. Unfortunately the Boss sailed in without buying a ticket for his companion. The boy had no money in his pocket at all. Fortunately he had a silver shilling on his watch-chain. He managed, after a struggle, to prise the shilling from the chain and sail in after his Boss to see the Show.

When he was somewhat older E.H. experienced an eerie event which has always remained vivid in his memory. He often used to pass a little cottage, now demolished for road-widening, which stood near Ley Mill and had a garden gate opening directly from the road. In this cottage dwelt a dear old soul with her only son, unfortunately a ne'er-do-well who was often seen the worse for drink. On this particular night, just as E.H. was about to pass the cottage, he saw quite clearly in the bright moonlight someone —

something — cross the road in front of him as though it were about to open the garden gate. It looked, E.H. told us, "like a big, black image wearing a black smock". But even while he was staring at it the image seemed to dissolve, to vanish into the shadows. Nobody was there to open the gate. E.H. continued on his way home considerably puzzled by his strange experience. He told no-one about it for fear that he should be laughed at. Yet a day or two later he heard that the ne'er-do-well son had died in the Bodmin Hospital at the precise time that he had been passing the cottage, exactly at 11.0 p.m.

Many of E.H.'s tales of his young days had, as their background, that rural way of life which has now utterly vanished, the days when Cornish villages were true local communities with a great sense of parish patriotism and when all the larger farmhouses had numbers of young chaps and maidens living in, who visited each others' farms and in spite of the long hours of work still had energy for a certain amount of rather rough horse-play and a great deal of innocent fun, including some fine singing. One such tale had, as its background one of the great annual Band of Hope celebrations that used to be held every June in Pensilva (St Ive) around the turn of the century and for many years thereafter. A mile race was open to all comers for the substantial prize of 7s 6d, a goodly sum in the days when a skilled farm worker earned only 15s 0d a week. The race was about to start when E.H. happened to come by in his working clothes. The competitors were already lined up, some of them from Plymouth wearing singlets and shorts and with proper running boots. "Come on, lad, you can run. Let's keep the money in the parish!" urged his friends. "I can't run in these great boots," E.H. objected. "Then take 'em off!" shouted his friends. So he did just that, rolled up his working trousers, discarded his jacket and ran the mile — three times around a grass field — in his stockinged feet. He won the 7s 6d.

In 1908 E.H. married a local girl, Mary Johns of Mount Pleasant, Pensilva, and, judging from the photograph I was shown, a very handsome young couple they made. Beginning their married life in a cottage with the traditional three acres and a cow, by hard work, and never missing an opportunity, they gradually bettered themselves. From employee E.H. graduated to employer, at one time employing twelve men cutting and drawing wood, removing bark for tanning, and taking it to the tannery at Launceston. He acquired more stock, and bigger farms until finally, in 1927, he settled in one of St Ive's finest farms, Haye Barton, and continued farming there until 1942. Then he retired with his wife to Pensilva and a son now farms Haye.

When E.H. was eighty-eight years old he decided the time was ripe to visit a sister long since settled in America. So he flew out to Chicago to a tremendous welcome and a wonderful family re-union. Smiling at my astonishment that he should take off into the skies thus, he remarked, "There was nothing to it. Nothing at all. I was looked after wonderfully well." It did not occur to him that few old gentlemen of that age go travelling about the world.

Ever since his wife died in 1962 E.H. cherished his independence and lived alone, latterly with a little discreet help from members of his family. I asked him where he had first met his wife. He thought hard for a moment and then shook his head ruefully, "Blessed if I know!" he confessed, at which we all laughed. Then he slid his arm along the back of my high wooden chair and with an innocent sideways look enquired, "And have YOU got a man my dear?"

I promised this fine old Cornishman that I would come to his next birthday party, as I had enjoyed this one so much. But it was not to be. E.H. died just a fortnight beforehand, full of years and honour. He had earned eternal rest just as surely as he had earned his first pair of Sunday boots. I count it a privilege to have met him.

Right: *Nicholas Roseveare, Quethiock's Postmaster for many years, who was very proud of his beard which he tucked inside his overcoat in windy weather. It was said to frighten horses and cause accidents. Nicholas played his accordion for most of the village dances and socials.* Below: *Mr Frank Pooley and his wife Isabel. He was the blacksmith at Higher Pounda and a jovial character to whose unofficial Maypole young people used to flock from miles around. On November 5th, he always went around the parish, knocking on doors and collecting, for some good cause.*

*Henry Bennett, blacksmith, of Blunts with two of his grandchildren, Lily and Ethel Jane, sisters of Bill Jane. The elder of the two died in 1976. The parish had three blacksmiths, vitally important, all kept busy in this farming community, and all three fine craftsmen. Photo c. 1890.*

# The School

Quethiock Voluntary Aided School, happily, still functions as the village school for the younger children. It stands in the centre of the village to testify to the importance that many good people attached to education long before the State realised its own duty in the matter. The school's oldest part is a simple stone-built, slate-roofed rectangle of some 30 ft by 14 ft, with stone chimneys at either end, and two windows on each side of a stone and slate-roofed porch. A somewhat later addition is an infants' room at the rear, and this was the whole school premises at the time of which I shall be writing. No water was laid on to the school. If the children's hands needed washing they had to go out to the nearest pump. If they were thirsty one child would man the pump while the rest, in turn, cupped their hands and drank. Toilet arrangements were primitive and the school stove, the only form of heating, frequently smoked. As many pupils had to walk miles to school in all weathers, often arriving wet through, this temperamental stove was necessary to dry their clothes, as well as heat the school, and warm the dinner-pasties.

Regular schooling for the children of the parish of Quethiock has an exceptionally long history. A school is first mentioned in 1811, when the Rev. John Kendall Fletcher had just become the new Vicar. In 1818 his successor, the Rev. John Rooke Fletcher, is also recorded as supporting a voluntary school for some thirty scholars, run on the monitorial system by a schoolmaster who received £15 p.a. Incidentally, John Rooke Fletcher remained Vicar of Quethiock for no less than sixty-two years, thus spanning the whole period, so vital to the education of the common people's children, between the time when village schools — where they existed — were purely charitable institutions and the time when the State had at last stepped firmly into the picture and by its School Boards Act of 1870 had created School Boards empowered to levy an Education Rate and to build schools where none existed. By this time Quethiock had its school, and the long record of parish education accounts for the fact that so many parishioners, as proved by the old parish registers, were able to sign their names when elsewhere the majority were only able to manage a pathetic, clumsy cross.

The modern era for education began, nationally, in 1832 when a Government Grant of 50% of the cost of building a school first became available to such societies as The National Society. The Church usually provided the balance of the money for building, while the maintenance and staffing was the responsibility of the parish. Quethiock had been quick to take advantage of this offer. On May 7th, 1840, a Deed, which granted "a piece of ground, a School House and Offices" in the village of Quethiock to John Rooke Fletcher, was signed by John Tillie Coryton of Pentillie Castle, "so that the Vicar or Curate could collect together such children of the poor inhabitants of the parish as the Trustees shall select for the purpose of educating and bringing up such children in the knowledge and practice of the Christian religion."

This first schoolhouse, the single storey room of 30 ft by 14 ft, was then considered adequate for up to eighty children, although there is a record of alterations and improvements in 1860. However, the School Boards Act of 1870 forced all villages to look critically at their schools and on 23rd November, 1874, Quethiock's School Log Book records that Mr Vincent, Architect, had visited the school and measured the interior, and further, that "The Ratepayers unanimously resolve that the Building forthwith be enlarged to meet the requirements of the Education Dept." In a Deed dated April 1st, 1876, Augustus Coryton, of Pentillie Castle, conveyed to John Rooke Fletcher, Vicar of Quethiock a parcel of ground, "for the purpose of a school", and by January 1877 the Log Book records that the schoolchildren were temporarily housed in a cottage while re-building was undertaken. So, at this time, a new room of 21 ft by 10 ft was added at the rear of the old one, which was the whole school premises at the time of which I write. A government measure which was important to the parish, was the Agricultural Children's Act of 1873 which stated that no child under eight could be lawfully employed in agriculture except on the farm of its parent or guardian and that a child under ten must make 250 school attendances in the year.

*Tea at the Vicarage for the children of the parish in August 1902, to celebrate the Coronation of King Edward VII. Mrs Wix, the wife of the Vicar, is the hatless little person in the centre of the doorway but elsewhere hats are very much in evidence, although some of the girls have been asked to remove theirs so that their faces can be seen. The boys, however, are sticking to theirs!*

Detailed records of the Quethiock National School begin in 1874, after the Revised Code of Regulations for National Schools had, in 1872, ordered that the Principal Teacher must enter in a Log Book facts concerning the school, its progress, dates of withdrawals, cautions, illnesses etc, "which may require to be referred to at a future time, or may otherwise deserve to be recorded", adding a warning that "no reflections or opinions of a personal character are to be entered in the Log Book." The first entry for May 1st, 1874, gives the result of H.M. Inspector's visit in February. "Considering the means at his disposal the Teacher deserves great credit for the results he produces. The room is too small and crowded, the furniture is cumbrous and not very suitable. There are very few books and no proper supply of maps and apparatus..."

Mr John Heddon, writer of this first Log Book, who received a salary of £12.10.0. a quarter, (Ellen Drown cleaned the school for 3s 6d!) remained the schoolmaster for the next twenty-two years and his record, in beautifully clear hand-writing, testifies to his real concern for the children in his charge and for their proper education. His first, chief, and most persistent trouble was absenteeism. Right away it is June, hay-making time, and his older scholars are taking to the fields to help save the hay in large numbers. This goes on until June 16th, when the whole school must have a day's holiday for Quethiock Band of Hope Festival. In July comes corn harvest and off his older scholars go again! This pattern of absenteeism in order to work in the fields runs through the whole of Mr Heddon's Log Book. He must have walked hundreds of miles chasing missing children, especially the worst culprits of all, the gamekeeper's children, who lived in remote cottages in the woods. Potato-planting was another educational hazard, so was the season for the taking up of turnips, and that for the sowing of seeds, but the chief hazard was the indiffference of so many of the parents. "There is not the interest taken by the Parents as should be, for the benefit of their children." The result was that whereas there might be seventy children on Mr Heddon's register only forty would be present.

Further, in the early years almost all the boys and girls left school as soon as they were twelve years old, or had passed the IVth standard. For example, in 1877 Mr Heddon writes, on April 25th, "Harry Riddle, William Cloke and Joseph Green leave school for work having passed the standards required, ages above eleven." We know that there was a happy sequel for little Harry Riddle, whose father had died when he was five, and whose mother had the usual hard struggle to rear her family. He went to work at Trehunsey for Mr and Mrs Hurrell, where he 'lived in', and I was told that he dearly loved Mrs Hurrell so she must have been kind to the little fellow.

In 1878 the long reign of John Rooke Fletcher as Vicar, and therefore Chairman of the School Managers, came to an end, and the new incumbent, the Rev. William Willimott, together with his wife and family, at once began to take an energetic interest in the school. He soon became a regular teacher-visitor and not only for scripture lessons but for other subjects, such as geography, in which he felt the scholars would profit from extra attention. In this same year a Report by H.M. Inspector of Schools stated that the infants were backward and required increased attention, suggesting that an assistant teacher should be appointed. Colonel Augustus Coryton, a Trustee, was a frequent visitor to Quethiock School, driving over from Pentillie with his sister, Miss Charlotte. He resolved the difficulty by paying the salary of an assistant teacher for the infant class out of his own pocket. Mr Willimott also helped Mr Heddon's labours by prodding the Committee into providing more infant readers, more maps and more books. Attendance slowly improved and in 1885 averaged 56. In 1891 the Great Blizzard is recorded, also the equally unusual fact that Herbert Cannon, a farmer's son, had left the school for The East Cornwall College in Liskeard. In September of this same year Mr Heddon was able to make an announcement that must have delighted his heart. For years he had complained that the school pence, of threepence per week, was a grievous burden upon the larger and poorer families, whose children were forced to leave after passing the IVth standard. Now he was able to anounce to the school, "as requested by the Committee", that their education would be free, although regular attendance would still be enforced. With the end of the school pence, the conspicuous pauper children, whose fees were paid by the St German's Board of Guardians, and who were the

*Mr David Champion, Master of Quethiock School, 1896 to 1914, outside the School House with his wife, who taught needlework. She looks a demure little person yet she could use her thimble as a painful deterrent against clumsy stitchery. Similarly, several of Mr Champion's punishments are still remembered – with feeling! Yet Quethiock School was renowned, for many years, for its exquisite needlework and for the excellent handwriting of most of its pupils.*

subject of visits from the Relieving Officer to check on their attendance, presumably merged with the rest. Entries such as this ceased to appear: "Admit Georgina Drown as one of the pauper children paid for by the Guardians of the St Germans Union."

Apart from their parent-instigated absenteeism Quethiock schoolchildren were surprisingly law-abiding. Their misdemeanours were very minor ones. Boys threw stones and broke windows, ate nuts in school, carelessly broke their slates and sometimes vanished from the playground to follow Colonel Coryton's hounds. Girls ran along the forms in the dinner-hour and one little miscreant actually refused to sing grace before dinner, "as requested", and so was kept in after school to write one hundred lines on her slate. However, the Log Book, as in this case, rarely records the actual punishment in detail, although it would seem that Mr Heddon never caned girls, but made up for it by caning boys with extra enthusiasm; he is reputed to have beaten some so soundly that he actually tore their clothes, which meant that they received a second beating when they arrived home. One of his terse and angry entries, in 1885, certainly boded ill for two of his flock, "William Kelly and Herbert Kelly sent IN DEFIANCE to Fair with sheep." One can almost hear the whacks!

In the later years Mr Heddon records names of children newly admitted to the infant class whom I knew in later life and who appear in my photographs. Blanche Snell of The Mason's Arms, who was admitted on October 15th, 1888, later became the Assistant Teacher, and is still, in 1977, able to talk about her schooldays. In 1889 two little sisters from Venn were admitted, Annie and Ethel Snell, the latter my mother-in-law, and also Jennie Harris from the village stores, who can still talk about her childhood. Mr Heddon's Log Book ended in April 1896, upon his retirement. No doubt his discipline was over-strict by modern standards. His little village school was cramped and poorly equipped. He taught what he, and the School Committee, at that time considered most essential, The Ten Commandments, The Twelve Times Tables, The Sermon on the Mount, Spelling — much of it repeated so often that even the dullest learned it for life. His own hand-writing was beautiful and so was that of many of his pupils. During his twenty-two years as Headmaster Mr Heddon never failed to point out the abiding value of education, not only to his scholars but to parents who were often indifferent, and in the early years even hostile. He certainly deserved his happy retirement in Rose Cottage, working in his garden which soon became a miracle of fruitfulness. At the time of the sale of the parish, when he was in his eighty-fifth year, Rose Cottage was only sold "subject to Mr Heddon being allowed to reside there free of Rent and all outgoings; the Property to be maintained in tenantable order for him by the Purchaser."

Unfortunately, the Log Book of Mr Champion, the Master who succeeded Mr Heddon, is lost. In this Log Book must have been chronicled the events which come within the memory of many parishioners. It may never be found. Even in 1899, the Rev. Augustus Wix, who had just succeeded William Willimott, was appealing for the return of the Vestry Minutes. They were never found, nor were several other parish documents. Therefore, for the time during which Mr Champion was Headmaster, I can only rely upon his pupil's reminiscences and the brief reports of H.M. Inspectors who usually rated his teaching as "vigorous and effective". For an authoritative record of this period I am forced to turn to the Log Book of the comparable, neighbouring Church School at St Ive. Immediately one is struck by the similarity. Absenteeism remains a problem. Even as late as July, 1916, Mrs Booth, Headmistress, writes, "Attendance only fair, many children helping in hay harvest and fruit-picking". The astonishing number of holidays and half-holidays continues. School still closes for St Matthew's Fair at Liskeard, for Callington Honey Fair, for various Temperance Festivals, and for many Church and Chapel Anniversaries. St Ive children, however, seem to be more badly behaved than those of Quethiock. In July 1919 Mrs Booth writes: "Had to punish Robert Hoskin for biting and kicking Miss Pearce" (Assistant Teacher). "He acted in the same way to myself so I punished him again." Even the Parish Councillors were badly behaved, for in January, 1917 Mrs Booth writes, with acid in her pen: "School used last night for meeting of Parish Council. This morning the floor was very dirty, men had been smoking and spitting, grating in front of stove broken into flooring, and pictures and postcards taken from walls, some torn, others thrown outside into yard."

*A group of schoolchildren in 1908. Miss Blanche Snell, daughter of Francis Snell, of the 'Mason's Arms' is the Assistant Teacher. She had entered the infant class, of this school, in October 1888, simply by crossing the road and she was still crossing it some twenty years later. Garfield Pooley, jolly son of Frank Pooley, was already taller than tiny Miss Blanche. Eileen Riddle, in a blue pinafore, stands beside Mr Champion. The children wear tough boots with nailed soles.*

Canon Hobhouse, Rector of St Ive and a great-grandson of the famous Bishop Trelawny, was yet another Victorian churchman who was a keen educationist. St Ive Church School had been completed in 1844 and Canon Hobhouse and his family always took a keen interest in it. In 1885 he wrote in the Log Book, "There is room for considerable improvement. To awaken thought ought to be strenuously aimed at. Reg. Hobhouse School Manager." No wonder he fathered Emily Hobhouse, of Boer War fame!

The very first old gentleman I visited, when I began my search for early reminiscences, had wonderfully sharp memories of his schooldays. Sitting by a crackling fire in his little cottage at Trehunist, next door to the one in which he was born, he chuckled with glee as he described how Mr Champion had once locked him, and his friend Bill Snell, in school in the dinner-hour, as a punishment. The two boys occupied themselves by writing on the blackboard:

> In Quethiock School
> There is a stool,
> And on that stool
> There sits a FOOL.

They then escaped by climbing through a window but qualified for a sound caning from a furious Mr Champion when school reassembled. He was, it would seem, an even stricter disciplinarian than his predecessor, while his demure little wife, who taught needlework, would hit the girls with a thimble until they cried. One of his nastier punishments was to keep a child standing for a long period with a pile of writing slates upon its head. These slates had heavy wooden frames and the slates were breakable. This punishment worried the good little girls far more than the tough little victims. Another frequent punishment was to hit small children hard under the chin so that their teeth rattled, very jarring and painful, so I was told. Nor were the girls immune. The big brother of one frightened small girl marched over to the school one day and told Mr Champion that if so much as a finger was ever laid upon little Winnie again then he would be right back to equalise matters. So Winnie was left in peace and today tells the story with a smile.

However, school life was not all tears and punishments. In summer the older children were perfectly free to picnic in the woods from mid-day to 1.30 p.m. and to play as they pleased. In autumn they would pick nuts and apples and eat them as 'afters'. In Mr Champion's day up to twenty children walked from Blunts to Quethiock every school day. Whenever a new infant started school an ancient pram, kept for the purpose, was fitted up once again with its 'pulling rope' and the older scholars took turns to pull-push the conveyance while the infant rode in style and comfort. In winter the dinner pasties were set to warm in a savoury-smelling circle on the top of the big stove. Here too steaming hot cocoa was brewed. After dinner games were played and the children sang or rehearsed for concerts. Winter was now very much concert-time, for both Mr Champion and the Rev. Augustus Wix were enthusiastic musicians who spent considerable time in organising village entertainments. Here is an account of a school concert held on Boxing night, Christmas 1901, in the Parish Magazine.

> On Boxing Night a packed audience appreciatively listened to school songs, recitations, etc., admirably selected and taught by the Master and Mistress (Mr and Mrs Champion). All the items were well rendered but especially "Dear Old Grandpa" by W. Snell; "Killarney" by Miss Champion; and "Come, Birdie, Come" by Miss Hancock. The Darkie Troupe was a great success.

This event was followed by another on January 10th, also reported in the Parish Magazine, when the schoolchildren first enjoyed "a substantial Cornish tea" and then a lantern entertainment, including "An Excellent Tale of a London Crossing Sweeper and His Two Sisters", and "Bob, the Shoeblack, or Honesty the Best Policy". Then came presents for all from the Christmas tree, both day school and Sunday school

*Quethiock School always celebrated May 1st with a formal Maypole Dance, usually held in a field adjoining. This, however, is a similar ceremony by neighbouring St. Ive scholars. The smaller girls weave the less complicated patterns with short ribbons, while the big girls, with much longer ones, have a more intricate task. Parental participation is obviously most satisfactory. Photo by Tom Harris of Quethiock around 1900.*

*Great excitement outside Quethiock School. Waggonettes are almost ready to depart for the Annual Outing to Looe, packed with scholars, parents and huge supplies of provisions. Embarkation is by stepladder. Although it is summer not a bare head or even a bare arm or leg is visible, c. 1900.*

scholars, each child receiving two gifts. Finally the Vicar begged the children never to be too proud to show respect to everyone. "He hoped that the good old-fashioned "touch of the cap" by boys and curtsey by girls would not be forgotten in this village."

In the same year, 1902, an Education Act was passed in October which set a great storm raging in East Cornwall. This Act, which was intended to be a progressive one, especially in that School Managers could be nominated by the new Parish Councils, was most bitterly opposed by many nonconformists. They contended that the Parish Councils were ruled by the Church and the big farmers, and that farm labourers dare not join them. They also resented the subsidising of Church of England and Roman Catholic Schools from the rates and many refused to pay their Education rate. Excitement rose to fever pitch when three men, one a Bible Christian minister, and the other two respected local citizens, were sentenced by Liskeard Magistrates on March 27th, 1905, to seven days imprisonment in Bodmin Gaol for non-payment. Like heroes they were accompanied to Liskeard station by a huge crowd, headed by the St Pinnock Temperance Band. *The Cornish Times* on Friday, March 31st, 1905, informed its readers:

> The three Liskeard 'Resisters' now in Bodmin Gaol will be released tomorrow, Saturday, about 7.30 a.m. They will be escorted to the railway station by Bodmin sympathisers and will catch the 8.30 a.m. train to Liskeard . . .
>
> They will be entertained to breakfast in the Temperance Hotel and in the evening there will be a public meeting in the Temperance Hall. During the week the 'Resisters' have been engaged in making bags for Post Office use.

The inflammatory nature of many articles written in nonconformist magazines must have made sad, even tragic, reading for many Rectors and Vicars who had over the years given generously of their time and their money in the cause of education. Here, for example, is part of an editorial in the Callington *Guild*:

> Are Methodists fully alive to the disastrous consequences that must ensue should the Education Bill become law? A clause denies popular control of schools. This means that at least 8,000 schools are left at the mercy of the Anglican priest, mostly village schools. Methodist children will be compelled to attend schools where will be taught, not religion, but a bastard Romanism . . . The very men who are looking forward to securing the control of the schools under this Bill are the very men who regard a thoroughly efficient standard of education as a national calamity. The unpardonable crime in the villages is that a labourer should even dare to have an opinion of his own. Local elections in villages are manipulated by the parsons and the landlords, very frequently with the connivance of the farmers. Parish Councils are in many places practically defunct. This would be to the taste of the Bishops who abused their position in the House of Lords by trying to prevent the creation of Parish Councils. God help England if the education of the rising generation is left to the most narrow, bigoted and unsympathetic of all the sects in this country – the Church of England . . .

And much, much more, including a call for Nonconformists "to resist to the uttermost the attempt to again shackle our nation with the chains of medieval and post-Reformation monkery and priestcraft."

The odd thing is that little Quethiock, at the centre of this whirling storm, remained totally calm. Relations between church and chapel folk remained tolerant and friendly. The children attended the church school in the week and on Sunday most came to the chapel Sunday school. All knew their Vicar as a familiar friend, and the very though of him shackling them with medieval chains was absurd.

This tolerance in religious matters was one of the reasons why Quethiock kept, even in this rather testing time, the reputation of being a happy village. Had it not been so, then the family life of Joseph and Fanny Wenmoth of Goodmerry would have been quite impossible for the five girls all attended church while the three boys joined the Wesleyans and all eventually married chapel girls.

*The Annual Band of Hope Festival in 1897. Eileen Riddle (see page 111) aged two, is in her father's arms, wearing a large white hat. Observe the many medals worn by both young and old.*

*The Mayor & Mayoress of Devonport come to 'open' one of Quethiock's famous Annual Flower Shows, first held in 1893 (see text). All the photographs of various flower show activities were taken around the turn of the century. It was said that the Mayor was reprimanded for wearing his splendid chain of office outside his borough, without permission.*

*Waiting for the speech, or perhaps the announcement of the show prizewinners.*

# Leisure

In Victorian Days Quethiock's main village street was a leisurely place, not merely a thoroughfare, but a kind of garden extension where villagers could stand awhile to gossip, and dogs, cats, toddlers, and even ducks and hens could roam in perfect safety. Older children could play here with tops, hoops and skipping-ropes, undisturbed except for an occasional farm cart or a pony and trap. Even the slowest old folk might creep across the road without anxiety, for the cows straggling home for milking, or Mrs Harris's grocery-delivering donkey, were pets rather than hazards. On summer Sunday evenings, after church and chapel were 'out', almost the entire village would stroll to and fro along the level piece of road between Yew Tree Corner and Trecorme, except for the young chaps who gathered in a group at Fool's Corner, where now the Parish War Memorial stands alone. Ironically, the great Yew Tree, the pride of the village, was cut down by order of the Devon Motor Transport Co., whose drivers found it a nuisance; today, Quethiock has neither ancient yew, nor any form of public transport.

It is in a peaceful and relaxed place that we must imagine the villagers, unharassed by cars and buses, as they go about their work and their leisure activities. The manner in which the parish was organised for work has now been described in some detail; it is time to take a look at what the parishioners did in their spare time. Today our chief leisure 'activity' entails no more effort than the pushing of a button and the drawing up of a chair. Formerly it was not so. Just as work was usually physically demanding, at any rate in the countryside, so also were most leisure pursuits. They were chiefly of that creative kind which by their very nature must involve much time and personal effort. Take, for example, the long preparation for Quethiock's famous Annual Flower Show. Every modern gardener will appreciate the months of work needed in order to produce first-class crops of flowers, fruit and vegetables. In the case of potatoes — which were of enormous importance to Quethiock's villagers and their pigs — then, as now, the gardeners were already picking out their seed potatoes for next year's crop as they harvested the current one. Then, too, there were the long preparations for choral concerts, dramas and penny readings, as well as regular cricket practice.

Furthermore, almost all the items sold at church and chapel bazaars were home-made or hand-made; home-made cakes, jams, pickles, butter and cream, hand-made crocheted doyleys, beautifully embroidered traycloths, pillow-slips and tablecloths. Weekly sewing parties were held regularly in preparation for the most important bazaars and when one bears in mind that these meetings, for church members, were commonly held in the Vicarage, a mile's walk from the village, and that many of the farmers' wives who attended had been up at dawn making butter, one can only be amazed at their toughness and enthusiasm. Similarly, the staunch cricketers were men who might well have walked miles to work and back, and been on their feet most of the day beside, yet they came to Bonker's Field for regular practice. Not for them the 'sadly barren excitement of vicarious living'. Parish-bound most of them were, but their lives were surprisingly full.

*An exhibition tent with no less than five judges and Mr William Roseveare, of Treweese, with them.*

*The tea tent with hostesses including Miss Flora and Miss Kate Wenmoth on the right. On the left are Miss Roseveare of Luccombe, Miss Bessie Kelly of Trecorme and Miss Edith Ryder who was the youngest of the eleven children brought up in the little Trecorme cottage on the hill.*

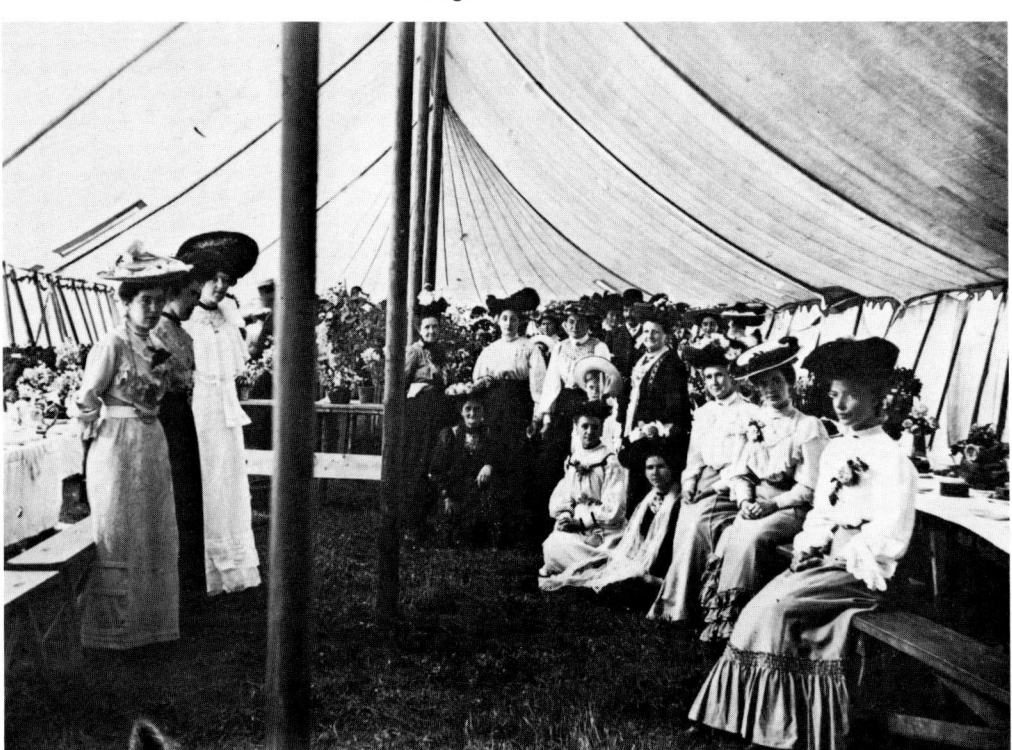

The Quethiock Annual Flower Show was a parish event of first importance, not only because it encouraged good food production but also because it engendered the keenest rivalry between parishioners, even within families, and so was a local focus of interest and a great talking point for many months together. This Show had begun in 1893, with Mr Heddon, the school master, its first energetic secretary, as reported in *The Cornish Times* of 22nd July.

Flower Show at Quethiock

The Show took place under the auspices of the Parish Institute, which is now in its fifth year of existence, and decided to hold the Show because the Pentillie Horticultural Society, having held 39 annual exhibitions, has ceased to exist. The classes were for Flowers, Fruit and Vegetables. Mr W. Coryton generously contributed to the Funds and the Show was a success. The Committee were as follows: Messrs Cannon, Hurrell, W Wenmoth, H Wenmoth, H Roseveare, G Riddle, E Kelly, J Harris, H Riddle, B Hawken. Mr J H Heddon acted as the Hon. Sec. of the Show.

The Callington Brass Band played. Miss Coryton and Master Jack Coryton of Pentillie attended the Show. The Public Tea at 5.0 p.m. was held under the trees below the schoolroom. During the day a cricket match was played by members of the Quethiock Club.

This first list of committee members, comprising farmers, farm workers, a carpenter, and the schoolmaster, is typical of the social mix found in all leisure activities. At this time there was only one 'private resident' in the parish, apart from the Vicar, a retired chemist who came of a very old local family, the Pollards of Trehunist. The Show was established as an annual event and soon began to attract many visitors from outside the parish. Mr Heddon always displayed some of his specialities 'not for competition' which included several varieties of apples, among which were Lord Suffields, English Stubbards, Early Jeannetons and Quarantines. The list of prizewinners grew longer and longer and there was always a brass band in attendance and a public tea. Family rivalry was acute from the beginning. Among prizewinners listed in the 1895 Show, under 'Cottager's Vegetables' were three brothers.

| *Class* | *Prize* | *Winner* | *Class* | *Prize* | *Winner* |
| --- | --- | --- | --- | --- | --- |
| Broad Beans | 2 | H Riddle | Potatoes, Kidney | 3 | T Riddle |
| Cabbages | 1 | G Riddle | Potatoes, Round | 1 | T Riddle |
| Leeks | 2 | T Riddle | Potatoes, Round | 2 | G Riddle |
| Peas | 1 | T Riddle | Shallots | 2 | T Riddle |

*Best Kept Garden under 20 yards*
| | |
| --- | --- |
| 1 | H Riddle |
| 3 | T Riddle |

After Mr Heddon retired in 1896 he devoted even more of his considerable energy to promoting the Show. He organised demonstrations of ambulance work, solicited prizes for the best teams of horses harnessed for ploughing, arranged the sports for children and adults and wrote postcards, in his beautiful handwriting, reminding all his friends to come to Quethiock Flower Show without fail.

Finally, here is the account of the 1900 Show, from *The Cornish Times* of July 28th.

*Francis Neil Snell, who was born in 1852 at the 'Mason's Arms', where his father, Edmund Snell, was the innkeeper. He died at 82 and was the last publican in Quethiock, for the hostelry closed in 1922 when his son, Bill, decided to revert to farming and surrendered the licence.*

*George Riddle, farm worker and sexton, surrounded by prize-winning potatoes. Born in 1858, he was an expert gardener who cherished his potatoes even to the extent of 'chitting' them under his four-poster bed at Well Cottages. Observe the button-hole, the pocket handkerchief, the gold watch-chain . . . and the PRIDE. He died in 1916.*

## Quethiock Flower Show

The Quethiock Flower Show was held on Wednesday, 25th, in a meadow near the Vicarage. The weather was delightful and there were many visitors to inspect the produce of parishioners' gardens, patronise the tea-tables and watch the sports which took place in the evening, while the Greenbank Band from Liskeard played merrily.

There were 260 entries, a committee of sixteen gentlemen, and two Hon. Secretaries. The Show was, as usual, held under the auspices of the Parish Institute of which Mr W Coryton of Pentillie Castle was President. The long list of prize-winners for flowers, fruit, vegetables and honey was divided into two classes, one, open to parishioners paying a rent of £5 p.a. or less who neither kept a horse nor cow, and second, all the rest.

Among the visitors were Miss Ruth Coryton and Miss May Coryton from Pentillie Castle and Mr C J Brooks, steward of the Pentillie Castle estates. In the evening there were sports for girls and boys, followed by a tug-of-war and a local steeplechase, for which the prize was a watch and chain.

A popular feature of almost every Flower Show was the cricket match. Quethiock had, for at least a century, a great reputation as a cricketing village. In one old account of the village I found this: "The happy spirit that makes Quethiock so attractive appears again in the Cricket Club. A more sporting set of men (and sporting in the finest tradition of the word) could not be found in Cornwall. Win or lose, theirs is a genial philosophy that so impresses opposing teams that they 'plump for Quethiock' when arranging fixtures a year ahead."

This record of a friendly match between Married and Single members of the Quethiock Cricket Club, shows a complete social mix of farmers, farm workers and craftsmen:

### Scores

| *Married* | | | | *Single* | | | |
|---|---|---|---|---|---|---|---|
| B Hawken | b | R Roseveare | 21 | Fred Snell | b | B Hawken | 7 |
| Frank Snell | c | Harris | | W Riddle | b | J Hawken | 9 |
| | b | Smith | 18 | R Roseveare | b | B Hawken | 3 |
| J Hawken | c | Snell | | H Roseveare | c | J Hawken | |
| | b | H Roseveare | 11 | | b | B Hawken | 5 |
| E Pollard | b | Riddle | 11 | H Wenmoth | b | B Hawken | 3 |
| W Higman | not out | | 5 | J Wenmoth | b | B Hawken | 5 |
| W Bennett | c | Snell | | J Harris | b | B Hawken | 0 |
| | b | R Roseveare | 0 | M Smith | not out | | 5 |
| J Bate | run out | | 4 | | | | |
| H Riddle | b | Riddle | 10 | | | Extras | 8 |
| | | Extras | 8 | | | Total | 45 |
| | | Total | 88 | | | | |

So the Married Men, thanks to the demon bowling of one of the village carpenters, Benjamin Hawken, won by a comfortable 43 runs and no doubt a hugely enjoyable time was had by all, including the spectators, for the whole village would turn out to watch a cricket match.

*The Flower Show Band. Don't miss the old gentleman who has got himself into the picture at the extreme left.*

*The Band of Hope Festival at St. Ive around 1912. The procession, preceded by a smart brass band and numerous banners, is forming up for its parade through the village. Caradon, the southern tip of Bodmin Moor (today topped by a television mast) is in the background.*

Not all the men of the village were pulsating with energy like the cricketers. There were some whose chief spare-time delight was to sit quietly by the fire in "The Mason's Arms" with a tankard of good beer before them. I have already mentioned this inn with its 19 acres of land, which made it the largest of the parish small-holdings, and also its hard-working mistress, Matilda, wife of Francis Snell, who bore six children in ten years and died in 1896 at 36. Francis Snell, part publican and part farmer in the good old tradition, was to be the last licensed victualler at "The Mason's Arms" for, in 1922, his son surrendered the licence and reverted to farming. By then business had obviously declined. For one thing Quethiock Cattle Fair, which had been held from time out of mind on the last Monday in January, finally petered out in 1894. Then, after the parish had been sold, the famous Audit Day dinner, when a baron of home-reared beef was always roasted, plus sides of pork, ducks and chickens, and dozens of meat and fruit pies baked, was ended. Older parishioners can still remember the excitement of watching all the farmers of the parish (with the one exception of Warren House) come driving into the village to pay their rents, and the even greater excitement of walking up to claim their own Rent Penny, which each child of the parish, by long custom, could do.

For many decades "The Mason's Arms" had a special reputation for excellent food, all home-produced. Many local firms would treat their most valued customers to a special dinner there. For example, a Tideford coal merchant, at Christmas, 1883, had sent a neat little printed card to all his favoured customers with this printed invitation:

Sir,
    The favour of your Company to Dinner at "The Mason's Arms", Quethiock, on Monday the 4th day of February, 1884 at One o'clock is solicited by
                                                       Yours respectfully,
                                                                Philip Blake

In the old parish registers Edmund Snell was always referred to as a Victualler, which means "One who furnishes provisions". Edmund was the father of Francis, who in turn carried on the tradition of good food. Probably the very strong temperance movement also gradually depressed the sale of alcohol and was yet another reason for closure, and the ending of a fine tradition of hospitality.

The temperance movement itself provided a focus for much leisure-time activity in the village. The great day of Quethiock's Band of Hope Festival was a Red Letter Day for almost all the children of the parish, church and chapel alike; among the adults the chapel folk were in the majority but there were a fair number of church members also. It was therefore a day of public jollifications, of exuberant hymn singing by the long processions that wound around the village carrying gay banners, Band of Hope members wearing medals, and the Rechabites, sashes. It was all tremendously exciting, and culminated in a splendid tea and a great evening open-air meeting, always attended by supporters from other parishes. Many bigger villages engaged a brass band to lead their processions. Pelynt, for instance, announcing its Festival for June 1883, promised that the procession would be headed by the Band of the 3rd Battalion, Duke of Cornwall's Light Infantry, followed by, "a great variety of ahtletic sports, a Public Tea and an Open Air Meeting." St Ive Band of Hope was headed by a smart brass band in 1912, thus continuing a long tradition, but Quethiock usually relied on its fervent hymn singing. Some of the hymns, like "Onward Christian Soldiers" are still familiar, but others are almost forgotten. In those days the special favourites were the simple Sankey hymns with catchy choruses such as:

        Ho, my comrades! See the signal waving in the sky!
        Reinforcements now appearing, Victory is nigh!

*Chorus*
        "Hold the Fort, for I am coming", Jesus signals still.
        Wave the answer back to Heaven, "By Thy grace we will."

*King George V Coronation Arch, at one entrance to the village, in August 1911. Two arches were erected, one at each end of the main street. Mrs Champion and Carrie Wenmoth are on the left.*

*Prize-winning teams owned by Mr William Roseveare. 1st. Harry Riddle's Team (he is wearing rosette). 2nd George Bennett's team.*

The singing was emphasised by much drum-beating and banner-waving. Another favourite was:

> "Go work in My vineyard, there's plenty to do;
> The harvest is great and the labourers few.
> There's weeding and fencing and clearing of roots,
> And ploughing and sowing and gathering of fruits.
> There are foxes to take, there are wolves to destroy,
> All ages and ranks I can fully employ."
>
> *Chorus*
> "Go work in My vineyard, there's plenty to do:
> Go work, work, work, work . . ." etc.

It is amazing how many old people remembered the words, as well as the chorus, of these old marching songs of the Church militant, very conscious of the fierce and subtle foe, but also completely confident of the final Victory.

The strength of the Band of Hope movement in the westcountry can be gauged by an account, in *The Callington Circuit Magazine* for 1902, of a major Temperance event which centred on Tavistock, in June, and in which 2,400 members took part.

> To see the various Bands of Hope entering the beautiful little town from all approaches was a very fine sight. One of the attractions was a vehicle decorated beautifully in flowers in various designs, which came with each society. Prizes were awarded for the best, and competition was keen. We can well picture a sturdy little Band of Hope setting out on its ten-mile drive in a decorated cart, with banners borne aloft by bright young faces (the men and women of the next generation). How it must have amazed and roused the curiosity of villagers and "passers-by" en route . . .
>
> After all the societies had gathered at the market a procession was formed and marched through the town accompanied by various bands and decorated waggons. A free tea, which kept sixty-four ladies fully occupied at the tables, and a great public meeting in the Town Hall, which was packed to its utmost capacity, occupied the remainder of a most successful day.

This single event, involving such large numbers, must have been very skilfully organised by people with a passionate belief in their cause. The numbers were not exaggerated. St Ive Band of Hope, in May 1902, numbered no less than a hundred members, "very creditable for such a little place", as the Circuit Magazine comments approvingly. Many other little places, including Quethiock, had almost as many. In towns, village villages and hamlets the thriving Bands of Hope met regularly for lusty hymn-singing and for the performance of recitations and plays which stressed the evils of over-indulgence in alcohol. Sober temperance addresses were craftily sandwiched between the more entertaining items, while tea and buns were never far away at the close. The extent and influence of the Band of Hope movement at this time cannot be over-estimated.

Quethiock had also another lively source of entertainment. The Parish Institute not only promoted the Annual Flower Show and the Cricket Club but also organised Socials and Dances in the village schoolroom for a variety of good causes. Music for dancing was usually provided by Nicholas Roseveare, the Postmaster, and his accordion. He was a venerable figure with a long white beard, more like the prophet Moses than a merry music-maker, and must have seemed a most improbable figure to be sitting sideways on the school platform, vigorously tapping time with one foot, squeezing away like mad, and shouting, "Come on, you boys, swing it! Swing it!" Nicholas was quite a character. At a time when everyone in the parish kept pigs he kept guinea-pigs. When asked why, his invariable answer was, "Because I like 'em."

These village dances were never attended by the Wesleyans, who disapproved of dancing as they also did of card-playing. However, they had many lively activities of their own, as is shown in the next section.

*Mr Alfred Harris, of the village stores, taking a day off at the seaside with his family. He is holding baby Winnie, the youngest of his ten children, and seven others are also here. Mrs Harris sits on a box beside him. Mr Tom Harris, his brother and a professional photographer, probably took the picture as his wife is seen on the left.*

# The Chapels

The modest size of the two plain little nonconformist chapels in the parish of Quethiock, one in the village and the other in the hamlet of Blunts, gives little indication of their influence and importance in Victorian days and beyond.

I have already mentioned the bitterness of the local controversy that preceded and followed the Education Act of 1902, a battle in which Quethiock appeared to take no part. This was not due to indifference, nor to any lack of understanding by the Wesleyans of their own distinctive doctrines, which emphasised personal salvation, an assurance bestowed upon them directly through faith in Christ. John Wesley, who had lived and died a clergyman of the Church of England, only wished to galvanise his church into new spiritual energy, not to found a new one. Yet his stirring proclamation that men should love God with their whole hearts, minds and strength, and should seek to proclaim and share the joyful news with their fellows, led to small groups of enquirers meeting in cottages and farmhouses in order to study this new and exciting teaching.

In Quethiock parish the first licensed nonconformist meeting-house was in the home of Samuel Tray in the village, also in the farm kitchen of Wisewandra, near Blunts. To these homes came the travelling preachers, men who worked at their trades during the week and walked or rode, often for many miles, in order to proclaim the good news on Sundays. This new emergence of spiritual enthusiasm in the parish coincided with the long sad decay of the church, which continued until Truro became a diocese in its own right in 1987. The Vicar, the Rev. John Rooke Fletcher, was eighty-eight years of age at the time, dying two years later. Dr Benson, first Bishop of Truro and later Archbishop of Canterbury, soon took the matter in hand but meanwhile, for many decades, the Methodists had provided a valuable spiritual witness in the parish, first in the two licensed meeting houses in private homes and later in their two newly-built chapels. By mid-century the parish church was becoming so ruinous that for many years such services as were held, were held in the school. Nonconformity filled the gap.

In 1836 the Methodist Conference had decided to ordain its own Ministers who could then administer the sacraments to the faithful, and dedicate themselves, like John and Charles Wesley, to the "spreading of scriptural holiness over the land." These men, after a period of training and probation, and having accepted the doctrines of Wesley's "Sermons" and his "Notes on the New Testament", were duly ordained and sent out as travelling preachers. Soon Wesleyan Methodist chapels began to spring up throughout Cornwall like mushrooms, the chapel in Quethiock village being built in 1839, and that in Blunts in 1843. Both stand today almost exactly as they were built, unpretentious witnesses to the piety and self-sacrifice of many humble folk.

At Blunts Chapel Jubilee in 1893 a special poem was written by a Mr T Higman to celebrate the historic occasion. It runs to no less than thirty-six verses on four sides of foolscap and in its own simple way bears moving witness to the enthusiasm and zeal of the builders of chapels such as this. Blunts, or Salem, chapel had been a Bible Christian cause until joining the Wesleyan Methodists in 1878. It must have been a very small society, for its first quarterly contribution to circuit finances was 2s 6½d, as compared with £17 19s 0d from Saltash. Here are some excerpts from the poem.

> Before eighteen hundred and forty-three
> Blunts was not as today we see.
> Very few houses were then to be seen
> And the people would worship in someone's kitchen.

*Blunts Methodist Chapel was built by the roadside, in 1843, on a plot given by John Snell, a local farmer, using the labour of its Bible Christian supporters. A stable was a necessity when preachers rode long distances to such small hamlets. Above the stable, reached from the back of the chapel, is a tiny gallery.*

*Blunts Methodist Church, as it is now called, decorated for Harvest Festival. A harvest rick stands before the table of offerings. On the wall behind the pulpit is a harvest sheaf and a scroll carved and painted in the 19th century by Mr Goodman, farmer, of Trevashmond.*

A man lived at Blunts by the name of John Dingle
Who thought that somehow they must have a chapel.
A man with the name of Snell was found
Willing to give a parcel of ground.

Thus having secured their wished-for site
They went in for building with all their might.
Some carted the stones and some mixed the mortar,
Each one seemed willing to help on his brother.

The walls a foot high, so the people say,
A man came to preach called Billy Bray
And this seemed to be the drift of his story
Christ in the heart is the hope of Glory.

Blunts then belonged to St Cleer Circuit
The Minister being one Mr Ebbett.
You will at once see how religion has ripened,
For then he had only ten pounds a year stipend.

His food would consist sometimes of porridge
Which he would receive in some labourer's cottage.
Sometimes he would get at the farmer's his fill,
And he has been known to work out in the fields.

At Luccombe I think was his principal stay.
There he would sleep three nights they say.
The friends there were kind, I would say, by the by
They would wash up his shirts, socks and neck-tie.

The poem then goes on to describe the appearance of the interior of the chapel as it used to be, with a lime-washed floor and a little round pulpit like a pill-box. There were high box-pews with doors, convenient to sleep in, but others would take snuff and then, "Hic, hic, Hem", the sleepers would presumably be awakened. Sometimes the cause flourished, sometimes not; once a preacher walked all the way from Stoke Climsland (ten miles each way) to preach to two people only. The poem describes how, very gradually, the little chapel was improved and a schoolroom and a stable built. It concludes:

Fifty years gone into eternity
The Spiritual work in full we can't see.
Souls have been saved and today they are found
Preaching Salvation to others around.

Friends, we thank you for coming today.
We thank you for helping our Bills to pay.
Please accept our thanks and allow me to mention
We want you to give us a splendid collection.

The emergence of the circuit system was of immense importance to Wesleyan Methodism and particularly so for its adherents in the small hamlets and villages. Wesley himself, in 1746, divided the whole country into seven circuits, of which Cornwall was one. As membership grew this Cornwall circuit was gradually divided and sub-divided until the Liskeard circuit was formed in 1809. Quethiock's Wesleyan Methodist society was accepted into this from its foundation and has remained with it ever since. Each circuit consisted of a number of societies grouped together under the pastoral oversight of the travelling preachers and later of the ordained ministers. One needs to call them societies rather than chapels because in the early years of the century so many preaching services were held in private houses, as at Wisewandra, near Blunts, where Edmund Webb, Circuit Steward and Class Leader, welcomed his fellow Methodists into his farm kitchen for services. The chapel at Blunts, after several changes of circuit, came to rest with Callington, so, therefore, from 1878 onward both chapels in the parish were Wesleyan Methodist, although in different circuits.

Because each chapel, however small, was always part of a much wider group of chapels it followed that all the local preachers, as well as those elected to attend the Quarterly Meetings and other circuit functions, were introduced to much wider responsibilities and met a more stimulating circle of fellow Christians than would have been possible in their own small societies. Local preachers, for instance, could only be accepted 'on trial' after an examination, mainly oral, by the Superintendent Minister of the circuit. After acceptance these men, some young, some old, some excellent preachers, some less so, travelled widely in the district and their varying approaches to prayer and scriptural teaching kept the local societies alert. One could say that while the Church of England slept in Quethiock, the Methodists were awake and busily discussing their doctrines. Both the Callington and the Liskeard circuits held frequent rallies for various good causes and these were well attended by the constituent chapels. In 1840 the Liskeard Circuit included twenty-three chapels with a total membership of seven hundred and twenty, although there were many regular worshippers who were not members. However, membership, here as elsewhere, fluctuated very widely over the years, swelling in times of revival and falling again as excitement faded. A solid core of the faithful always remained, so that the circuits could, and did, play an extremely important role in the further education of many village people at a time when the state was only beginning to acknowledge its responsibility in the matter. Over the years many men raised in the Wesleyan tradition, both in Callington and Liskeard, became leaders in their communities and played an active part in parish and district affairs. Louis Harris, for example, (1884-1973) the miller at Trecorme before the great Sale, after which he bought Ley Farm in St Ive, served as a Liskeard Rural District Councillor for twenty-five years and he was but one of many such faithful servants to the community.

As the nonconformist chapels grew in strength and influence during Victoria's long reign so their 'nonconformist conscience' became a force to be reckoned with. I have already described the temperance movement and the Band of Hope, supported by many members of the Church of England. Total Abstinence, on the other hand, was a peculiarly Methodist cause which grew powerful only in the second half of the century. Liskeard Wesleyan Church (the word 'chapel' is no more used) still has a wine cupboard in its vestry, formerly used for the refreshment of its preachers, who were offered a glass of wine before and after the service. Barrels of beer were formerly provided also for the all-day Liskeard circuit Quarterly Meetings. At first the Total Abstinence movement was strongly opposed. In 1839 not one chapel in Liskeard would allow the Total Abstinence Society to hold a meeting on its premises and even the Town Council refused the Society the use of the Town Hall, which leads to an incredible but perfectly true story. Mine Host of "The Bell", an old Liskeard coaching inn, heard of the Society's difficulty and — possibly with his tongue in his cheek — offered it a room in the inn. The offer was accepted, so here, in this most unlikely place, the first Total Abstinence meeting was held and the first pledges signed. Mine Host proved to be an ill friend to many of his fellow publicans for members of a respected local family, the Tamblyns of St Pinnock, were among those who signed their pledges in "The Bell". Later, in 1866, they founded the St Pinnock Band of

Quethiock Wesleyan Methodist Chapel was built in 1839 and is unchanged today. The fine ironwork on the door and elsewhere was probably designed and made by the Hawkens of Treweese. They were certainly working there for in 1838 William Hawken, aged 24, son of Richard Hawken, blacksmith, of Treweese Cross, married Sarah Ough, 24, daughter of William Ough, mason. In 1919 there was still a Hawken, blacksmith, at Treweese and an Ough, mason, at Birch Hill.

This interior of Quethiock Methodist Church was taken about 50 years ago. At the turn of the century a little chapel, such as this, would have five meetings on Sundays, as well as a Class Meeting and a Prayer Meeting in the week. A Band of Hope also met every week in winter.

Hope which became so influential that all four public houses in the neighbourhood closed for lack of trade. Eventually no less than nine parishes in the Liskeard area had not a single public house between them. A surprisingly high proportion of the older generation are total abstainers to this day.

Wesleyan Methodists from the first founding of their societies gave particular attention to the religious education of their children and devoted much time and care, and a high proportion of their limited funds, to the Sunday Schools. The Sunday Schools at Quethiock village and Blunts were for many decades large and flourishing and attended by most of the children in the parish whether their parents were Methodists or not. The Sunday Schools were bright and attractive gatherings, whose scholars qualified for pretty cards with texts, for merit and attendance prizes, and for special parties and treats. These were the sprats to catch the youthful mackerel who came in shoals to sing hymns written specially for them. In 1763 the Wesley's *Hymns for Children* was published. Other special volumes of hymns for children followed. The *Wesleyan Methodist Sunday School Hymn Book* of 1879 would have been the one used in Quethiock's chapel Sunday Schools until 1911, when *The Methodist School Hymnal* was published. The children's singing was always a very special feature of the Sunday School Anniversary, usually held at Whitsun, when the scholars, in smart new clothes, read the Lessons, gave recitations and solos, and all sang the specially rehearsed hymns to chapels packed to more than capacity. It was a poorly attended Sunday School Anniversary at the turn of the century that had no chairs in the aisles and extra forms at the rear.

Unfortunately no records of these events can be traced in the parish, apart from the vivid memories of older people. Fortunately the records for a comparable Sunday School, that for Downgate, not far distant, survive in the County Archives. In 1906 Downgate Sunday School had 140 scholars, 26 teachers, 2 Superintendants, 2 Assistants, plus a secretary and a treasurer, a total of 172 persons. There was also an Adult Class of 40. These very large numbers in a small community can probably be explained by the fact that almost all the children and young people came to the Methodist Sunday School.

The Anniversary Day was always closely followed by the Sunday School Treat, in the early days held in a field lent by a local farmer. Trestle tables and forms were set out to which the children brought their own plates and mugs and tremendous appetites. There were games and sports and prizes for everyone. Later, farmers cleaned out spring wagons, both in Blunts and Quethiock, and took the children to the seaside. Not for them the excitement of going by train, as Liskeard scholars did in 1860, travelling on the new line to Lostwithiel! Here is Downgate's Financial Statement for both Anniversary and Treat in 1910.

### May 1910 Sunday School Anniversary

| *Receipts* | £ | s | d | *Expenditure* | £ | s | d |
|---|---|---|---|---|---|---|---|
| Balance from last anniversary | 1 | 19 | 6 | Paid for provisions | 1 | 19 | 0 |
| Sunday Collection | 1 | 17 | 8 | Paid for butter and cream |  | 9 | 6 |
| Monday Collection | 1 | 7 | 9 | Paid Mr Maker for printing | 1 | 3 | 0 |
| Taken at Tea Tables | 3 | 4 | 0 | Paid Mr Hicks for Boiling Water |  | 4 | 6 |
| Provisions Sold |  | 5 | 3 | Paid Sweets and Nuts for Children |  | 5 | 0 |
| Hymns Sold |  |  | 7 | Paid Prov. for Teacher's Tea |  | 7 | 3 |
| Hymn Books |  | 5 | 0 | Paid Sunday School Hymn Books |  | 4 | 3 |
|  | 8 | 19 | 9 | Paid Roll Book |  | 1 | 0 |
| Taken | 7 | 17 | 4 | Paid Rewards for Children | 3 | 3 | 10 |
| Balance | 1 | 2 | 5 |  | 7 | 17 | 4 |

Another distinctive Wesleyan Methodist tradition was its strong support for overseas missions. Very early in the life of the Liskeard circuit it had taken to heart the injunction, "Go ye into all the world and preach the gospel to every creature." As early as 1815 a series of missionary meetings had been held in Liskeard "which the pious and benevolent of every denomination were requested to attend." After these meetings in the Methodist Chapel a circuit missionary society was formed, which Quethiock joined. Benjamin Carvosso (1789-1854) was one of many men connected with Liskeard who became missionaries. He went to New South Wales in 1820 and helped to found the first religious magazine in Australia. William Lawry went out at about the same time and in 1843 became General Superintendent of Wesleyan Missions in New Zealand. The missionary tradition continued and strengthened throughout the century. Dr Roderick McDonald, for a time assistant to a Methodist practitioner in Liskeard, went out to China as a medical missionary in 1884 and was murdered by pirates in 1907. Little rural Quethiock, tucked away in its green lanes, because its small chapel was part of the wider Liskeard circuit, was therefore closely involved with far away places, with Australia and New Zealand, with India and Ceylon, with Tonga, Fiji, China and many others. Regular collections were made, both in chapels and Sunday Schools, for overseas missions, and when men and women missionaries returned home on furlough they described the countries in which they laboured and the people to whom they ministered to large and appreciative audiences at circuit rallies. No intelligent village child could be unaware of the world overseas. No intelligent adult could be unaware of the challenge to Christians. They all knew Isaac Watts' famous hymn:

> Jesus shall reign where'er the sun
> Doth his successive journeys run;
> His kingdom stretch from shore to shore
> Till suns shall rise and set no more.

By the end of the nineteenth century most Wesleyan chapels in the Callington and Liskeard circuits were holding weekly 'Guild' nights, partly devotional, partly educational. Liskeard Wesley chapel, in 1890, had also a Young Men's Institute and a Mutual Improvement Society, where mathematics, shorthand and English were taught. There was also a flourishing gymnastic class. The Sunday School, which was only one among several others in this small town, numbered three hundred and sixty scholars and thirty-four teachers. The influence on the whole community must have been tremendous.

Methodism, it is said, was born in song, and hearty congregational singing has always been a distinctive part of its worship. Cornishmen, like the Welsh, dearly love to sing and so hymn singing has always brought deep joy to Cornish hearts. Charles Wesley gave his followers some wonderful new songs to sing, such as "Christ, whose glory fills the skies," and "Jesu, lover of my soul". For the little children he wrote:

> Gentle Jesus, meek and mild,
> Look upon a little child.
> Pity my simplicity,
> Suffer me to come to Thee.

The great majority of Methodists in Victorian days were thoroughly familiar with their Hymn Book and knew a great many hymns by heart. Moreover, they sang them, not only at home or in chapel, but out in the fields, working in the cowsheds, wending their way homeward along the evening lanes. Many Methodists

*Blunts Chapel Sunday School outing to Downderry in 1900. The farm wagon belongs to Mr Goodman, who is holding the reins, while the man with the beard is Mr Tobias Higman who wrote the poem recited at the Chapel Jubilee in 1893.*

*Mr William Jane, in 1976, holding the model harvest rick made by his father nearly a hundred years ago. It has three distinct bands of straw, oats, wheat and barley, it is properly thatched with reed and spars, and has staddle-stones at the four corners.*

enjoyed the new Sankey Hymns, popular tunes with repetitive choruses, some of which were of doubtful spiritual or musical value, hymns that John Wesley might well have deplored as rarely having the "purity, strength and elegance" that he desired of a hymn. However, when a group of chapels met together for evangelistic singing, as they frequently did, some would choose from Wesley's own collection "for the use of the people called Methodists", while others would prefer hymns chosen by Ira Sankey. Not all of these were ephemeral. The swinging, "Blessed assurance, Jesus is mine, Oh what a foretaste of glory divine," with its chorus, has brought joy ever since it was written, – by a woman who had lost her sight at six weeks old. So, whether they sang fine poetry set to noble music, or simple words set to popular tunes, or a mixture of both, the Wesleyan Methodists in Quethiock sang joyfully and whole-heartedly, "Speaking to one another in psalms and hymns and spiritual songs, singing and making melody with your heart to the Lord."

Here, in his own words, are some reminiscences of a fine old gentleman, born in 1893, who was brought up in the best Methodist traditions and has remained faithful to them all his long life.

> My father, Thomas M., went to farm service at nine years of age at sixpence a week and his food. By thirteen he was driving a pair of horses with a butt wagon, moving soil when the Holsworthy railway line was being built. He became a farm labourer and later married on fifteen shillings a week, less two shillings and sixpence for house rent. He was a good, steady worker and was soon promoted foreman at Haye, and stayed on that farm for nearly seventeen years. Here six of my brothers and sisters were born. Meanwhile all our family were saving hard to be able to rent a farm of our own. My mother milked eight cows morning and evenings for four shillings a week – a seven day week. After milking she had to hurry home to fry the breakfast for our lodger, who carted the Squire's milk from various farms to be sterilised before going to Plymouth. Her 'milk money' and her 'lodger money' was all carefully put away in the 'Farm Fund'. So was any money earned from fruit-picking, including ours. Mother would earn three shillings a day picking gooseberries, we children would get about half that.
>
> While I was still at school we had a plague of rats in the district and Squire offered a penny for every rat killed. I got busy right away in the culverts and caught three-hundred. Squire was pretty astonished by the number, but didn't disbelieve me, and paid up. However, I cut the tails off all the rats I caught afterwards, and brought them along in bundles of twenty-fives. This was a fine help to our Farm Fund, especially when you remember that at the turn of the century you only got six shillings for making a hundred faggots and three shillings an acre for spreading farmyard manure from heaps, a day's work for most men. We lived as much as possible off the land. Father now had nineteen shillings a week for working from 4.45 a.m. to 5.0 p.m. and being responsible for eighty cows. There was mother's money, and we children began to be useful. We saved what we could, but we always had enough to eat and to wear and were a happy family.
>
> One morning, Edith, my oldest sister, and I came downstairs to find our mother crying. She was crying with joy and told us that Father had been converted the night before at a Mission Meeting. I rushed out to the cowhouse to see what had happened to him. He was washing the cooler before breakfast just as usual, except that he was singing,
>
> > Sweeping through the gates of the New Jerusalem
> > Washed in the blood of the Lamb.

From then on we had prayer meetings in the home, and singing, with men coming in from the surrounding farms and hamlets in the evening. Edith learned to play the piano and we had some wonderful singing. In 1908, at Ladyday we moved as a family to our own farm, having saved about £400, which was quite a nice start in those days. We could never have saved it if father had been a drinker and a smoker. We were taught verses as children that I can still remember. I recited this at a Temperance Meeting when I was about five or six.

### The Noblest Plan

That unhealthy old weed
That true women detest
And all people know
Is a filthy old pest.

They are foes to all virtue
They lead down to shame.
Shun drink and tobacco
And keep a good name.

Cold water that comes from
The well is my drink.
The healthiest, purest
And sweetest, I think.

It never makes drunkards,
It never brings woe,
So I'll praise it and drink it
Wherever I go.

I will end by giving a list of the Quethiock Chapel Trustees just before the Sale in 1919, names that may now be familiar.

| Local Trustees | | |
|---|---|---|
| | Thomas Vosper | Farmer, Haye |
| | Alfred Harris | Grocer, The Shop |
| | Alfred Snell | Farmer, Venn |
| | Richard Wenmoth | Farmer, Hepwell |
| | Wilfred Wenmoth | Farmer, Great West Quethiock |
| | Louis Harris | Miller, Trecorme |
| | Benjamin Hawken | Carpenter, Treweese Cross |
| | Sydney Hawken | Carpenter, Treweese Cross |
| | Joseph Wenmoth | Farmer, Goodmerry |

There is a fitting footnote:

At the Annual Meeting of Trustees of Quethiock Wesleyan Chapel Trust held on Feb. 16th, 1921 it was resolved, "That we express our thanks and appreciation to the Trustees of the late William Coryton for the gift of freehold of land. Noted that the Deed of Transfer being duly signed and examined by the General Chapel Committee and now deposited in the Circuit Safe."

*This fine Celtic Cross (8th-9th Century) stands in the churchyard near the ancient well by which Saint Cadoc is reputed to have preached. It rises 13ft 4 in. above ground, an incised granite wheel-head cross that is one of the best preserved in Cornwall. The church tower is also unique. Built as a continuation of the church gable end, it rises from the roof, not from the ground, and is therefore unusually tall and slender. Access to the upper storeys is by a short staircase turret.*

*To left and right are brass rubbings taken from the chancel floor. These are from the effigies of Roger Kyngdon of Trehunsey, who died on the 3rd of March AD 1471 and also of his wife Johanna. The inscription, in Latin, ends, "On whose souls Jesus may have mercy, Amen."*

101

# The Church

Quethiock Church has now stood for over six hundred years as a visible witness to Christian parish history, a building which is a proud and unique inheritance. The tall Cross standing close by in the Churchyard is an even older witness.

Here, in the beginning, was only a clear stream running through a south-sloping meadow. Then the Celts who dwelt in this fertile place dug themselves a well, and to this well came a travelling missionary priest from Wales called Cadoc, who celebrated the Christian Mass here in the open air. He became, later, a Celtic saint and the Patron Saint of Wells. Soon a small shrine was built for the missionary priests who followed him and who, like Cadoc, preached in the open air. Then, in the eighth or ninth century, the beautifully incised granite wheel-head cross was erected, 13 ft 4 ins above ground and one of the finest and tallest in Cornwall. It stood here for some eight hundred years until it was pulled down (though some think it was taken down and hidden for safety) during the Reformation period. Thereafter it was lost for centuries until found, in three pieces, but all of them perfect, in 1881, and reverently re-erected. This splendid Celtic Cross is therefore about twelve hundred years old and a treasured parish Christian heirloom. Later a small, simple Saxon church was probably built close by the Cross, to be superseded after the Conquest by a cruciform Norman building in stone. In 1288 this first Norman church, which like the earlier Saxon one had been dedicated to St Cadoc, was re-dedicated to the French saint, St Hugh de Avalon. However, the people of Quethiock clung fiercely to the memory of their Celtic saint, and Quethiock Fair Day continued to be held on the last Monday in January, thus commemorating St Cadoc's Feast Day, which is January 24th in the Celtic Calendar, right up until 1894, when the Fair came to an end. In 1336 the church was appropriated to the Arch-presbytery at Haccombe, Devon and in 1344-6 it was entirely rebuilt just as it stands today, except for the addition of a south porch and a north aisle in the following century. This north aisle covers most of the older north transept except for the last five feet, which remains as evidence of the original cruciform building. The curious slender tower, which rises up from the roof, is unique.

Much evidence still remains inside the church to remind parishioners of the medieval days when western Christendom was one and undivided. Indeed unless one does understand that this was built as a Catholic church, primarily as the shrine in which daily Mass was celebrated, but also as a building whose nave and porch had many important secular uses, then some of the internal arrangements must seem — to say the least — odd. What, for example, can be made of a stone staircase that winds upward in the thickness of a wall only to end in an open aperture? Nothing, unless one knows that this staircase once led to a great beam across the church upon which stood the images of Our Lord on the Cross, with Our Lady and St John on each side. Below the Holy Rood candles always burned, which the Parish Clerk must tend daily, hence the need for the Roofloft staircase. Similarly the piscinae, and the stoup for holy water by the south door, with much else, can only be understood in the light of church history.

These ancient reminders are all that survive from the medieval days when this parish church, like all others, was glowing with brilliant colour, its windows full of vivid stained glass, its walls painted with dramatic murals, the many statues coloured and gilded, even the roof decorated with bright angels and roof-bosses. Here in Quethiock, in medieval days, the transepts held the painted effigies of the Lords of Trehunsey and Trecorme whose money had paid for building them. The Lord of Trecorme also had a chapel on his own land in 1434, and there was a field called 'Pope's Field' in 1842, at the Tithe Apportionment.

*The Mission Church at Blunts, demolished in 1976. A brass tablet taken from it and now in St. Hugh's vestry reads:*
   *'Blunts Mission Church, Erected in Memory of CHARLOTTE CORYTON, Died 16th October 1899. by William Coryton of Pentille Castle, 1902.'*

*Interior of St. Hugh's, probably taken in 1905 after the new organ had been installed. A former Vicar, the Rev. W. Willimott (1878-1888) had, with his own hands, restored the church to much of its ancient glory, designing and making stained glass windows, carving new woodwork and renewing much else beside.*

The nave was the parish meeting place, the centre of community life; because the church was dominant in all secular matters, the law meant ecclesiastical law, charity meant church charity, insurance against misfortune meant membership of one of the Guilds which met here. The same candles which lit up the Rood and shone down upon this busy scene must also have illuminated the splendid brass effigy of Roger Kyngdon, his wife, and his eleven sons and five daughters. The Latin inscription is: "Here lie Roger Kyngdon, Johanna his wife, sons and daughters, and all their progenitors, who died the 3rd day of March, A.D. 1471. On whose souls Jesus may have mercy. Amen." Roger must have been a small man for his effigy is cunningly heightened to match that of his wife by standing him upon a little mound. The Reformation, with all its tragic unheaval, separates this medieval brass from another on the wall of the Trehunsey transept, placed there in memory of Richard Chiverton who died in May 1617. The Trehunsey brass is in the nave, close by the Rood loft staircase, but by 1617 there was no Rood and no candles, for in 1547 the King had decreed that all Roods and other images on the Rood gallery, and elsewhere in the church, must be removed and the walls whitewashed. The Kyngdons and the Chivertons held Quethiock manors which later passed to the Corytons, illustrating the long continuity of land ownership in the parish.

The post-Reformation history of St Hugh's, which after the final break with Rome was largely dictated by national and parliamentary policies, must be passed over swiftly in order to come to the late Victorian period with which I am chiefly concerned. Two matters of local interest should perhaps be mentioned, the erection of endowed almshouses in 1633 by Walter Coryton for four poor spinsters, and the Tithe Apportionment of 1842 after which Tithes in kind were replaced by money payments. The levy on the parish of Quethiock was £686, half still going to the Rector of Haccombe and the other half to the Vicar. The long, sad decay of St Hugh's, both physical and spiritual, was splendidly halted by the Rev. William Willimott, Vicar from 1878 to 1888, who worked diligently to restore it to some of its ancient glory. At this time there were many other Anglican churchmen who felt their identity with the ancient undivided church, who wished to revive some of the lost emphasis on the Sacraments, and to restore beauty and dignity to church services.

William Willimott came to a bare, ruined church with sagging pillars and a leaking roof. He carried out a thorough restoration including much of his own new carving in oak, and the designing and making of many fine stained glass windows from his Vicarage workshop. So, in a north window, St Cadoc is preaching by the ancient Cross and a chancel window depicts St Hugh with a tame swan. This craftsman's work was not all carried out immediately, but as soon as the church had been made safe and weatherproof it was re-opened in 1879 by the first Bishop of Truro, Dr Benson. Colonel Augustus Coryton presided at the luncheon which followed and enough money was given that day to pay off the outstanding debt completely. William Willimott, who worked so hard to restore St Hugh's to some of its former beauty, was soon to be followed by yet another outstanding man in the same tradition.

Augustus Wix, Vicar from 1899 to 1907, was a priest who gave himself completely to the church and his parish. The List of Church Service as given in the Parish Magazine for February, 1902, is in startling contrast to the laxity of earlier times. (One cannot but regret that many more men like William Willimott and Augustus Wix had not been active in the church when Wesley was doing his best to revive it, for after all, Wesley had said, "I live and die a member of the Church of England, and none who regard my judgement will ever depart from it." Alas, by the time William Willimott was carving his screen it was already fifty years too late, for the Methodists were ordaining their own Ministers, and in Quethiock their chapels had been built.)

Quethiock Parish Magazine for February 1902

List of Services

Sundays          1st and 2nd Sunday. Morning 11, Matins, Sermon; 11.45 Holy Communion. Evening 6.30, Evensong, Litany, Sermon.

3rd, 4th and 5th Sundays. Morning 8.0 a.m., Holy Communion; 11, Matins, Litany, Sermon; 6.30, Evensong, Sermon.

Saints' Days     M., 8.0 a.m., Holy Communion

Daily            8.45 a.m., Matins; 6.30 p.m., Evensong, 5.0 p.m. in the winter months.

The church is always open for Private Prayer.

Vicar: J Augustus Wix

Augustus Wix was a keen musician who desired a good organ in the church to the greater glory of God. Also he was yet another Vicar not afraid to use his hands. In order to raise funds for the desired new organ he made walking sticks and carriage whips and sold them at local fairs and markets. The children sang:

> Parson Wix, Has giv'd up playing organ,
> And gone selling sticks.

Another local rhyme went thus:

> Bazaars and all their devious tricks,
> Disgust our honest Parson Wix,
> So in the woods he goes and picks
> Himself some hundred walking sticks.

Whether he was disgusted by Bazaars or not, the honest Parson had to endure these inevitable money-raisers. *The Cornish Times* of February 6th, 1904 describes one such event:

A Quethiock Sale of Work

Aiding the Church Organ Fund

Mrs Coryton, who had driven over from Pentillie Castle to open and assist the sale, expressed her pleasure in coming to the village to open the Shop.

Then follows a long list of the stall-holders, ending with the announcement that the sale had made £37. An evening concert followed at which Mr William Maddever sang, "Measure your wants by your means," with the encore, "The Union Jack". Other village artistes also contributed, with piano and harmonium playing. Comic songs and duets were sung, and there was a further useful contribution to the Organ Fund. Of course the target was eventually reached, the Vicar was able to have a specially fine organ installed, and in his day church music flourished. It was he who had the three church bells — known as Kettle, Crock and Pan — rehung. Thereafter they were rung by the three Riddle brothers although, when necessary, George Riddle could manage to ring all three by himself, two with his hands, and one by a foot in a loop. George Riddle also rang the village curfew every night at 8.0 p.m., until the outbreak of the first world war. There is a brass memorial to him in St Hugh's which says:

> To the Glory of God and in Affectionate Memory of
> George Riddle
> who served this church faithfully for 32 years.
> At Rest. Jan. 5th, 1916.
> Peace, Perfect Peace.

The Rev. Augustus Wix also discovered the lost parish stocks and had them placed in the church porch. They have six holes. He must have possessed quite extraordinary stamina for, in addition to his many church services and his duties in the village school and in the parish generally, he formed a "Glee Class" which rehearsed and performed concerts and 'Penny Readings'. Here is an extract from the Parish Magazine describing one such event:

### Penny Reading

The Vicar's Glee Class, formed a few weeks ago, gave a short entertainment on Thursday, January 16th consisting of songs, glees and readings. For One Penny the audience heard the following programme: National Anthem; glee, "O, who will o'er the Downs so free"; song, "The Waggoner" (Mr H Riddle); "Tarnham Toll" (Miss C Olver); reading, "Our Village" (Mr Champion); glee, "Sing we and chaunt it"; song, "Three Sailor Boys" (The Vicar); glee, "Come o'er the brook, Bessie"; reading, "The Mistletoe's Advice" (The Vicar); patriotic song and chorus, "True to England and her King" (Mr I Hawken); song, "My Moke" (The Vicar)". An excellent pennyworth!

The Vicar, however, was not all songs and smiles, far from it. He could speak his mind very forcibly when he felt that it was necessary. One such occasion was when he wrote about his "Living" of Quethiock. The italics are his own.

Many persons still have the idea that the "parson" of the parish always has a long "purse" at his command arising from the Tithe Rent Charge and rents of Glebe Lands. However "fat" other livings may be, the Vicar of this parish would like his parishioners to cast their eyes over the following statements, so that they can judge for themselves whether the income of his living can fairly be termed a "fat" or a "lean" one:

*1899*

| *Incomings* | £ | s | d | *Essential Outgoings* | £ | s | d |
|---|---|---|---|---|---|---|---|
| Tithe Rent | 232 | 1 | 1¾ | (all named and including | | | |
| Charge Glebe Rent | 29 | 0 | 0 | Poor Rates and Land Tax) | 57 | 2 | 5 |
| | 261 | 1 | 1¾ | | | | |

**TOTAL NET INCOME £203 18 8¾** (*not* including subscriptions)

This particular piece was written for the Parish Magazine, but a sharp "Notice from Vicar" might sometimes appear in the Deanery Magazine, as for example this, about the erection of tombstones:

*A Looe that has vanished since 1905 when the Church Choir visited it for their Annual Outing. The Vicar has stood on the Banjo Pier with his camera to record the event. On the beach sit the choir members and friends with tea kettles and hampers of provisions as seaside amenities were virtually non-existent. The small girl (front left) is Eileen Riddle and, next to her, reclines Mr Heddon, the retired schoolmaster, with his successor, Mr Champion. Far right, is Mr Champion's son, Bruce, who was killed in the First World War.*

*Walking sticks and carriage whips fashioned by the Rev. Augustus Wix from hazel wood cut in Digoridge Wood. These were sold at local fairs and markets for the Church Organ Fund and the effort was crowned with success in 1905, the acquisition of a fine new organ being acknowledged as a 'personal triumph for the vicar'.*

The Rev. J. Augustus Wix, Vicar of Quethiock from 1899-1907, relaxing outside his kitchen window. An energetic parish priest, he was also a keen musician, naturalist, cricketer and amateur photographer to whom we owe many of our illustrations for this book.

Violet and Nancy, daughters of the Rev. Wix, who were both born while their father was Vicar of Quethiock. Nancy is the younger of the two. Their charming nursemaid is Miss Emma Cloake, a girl from the village, whose father is seen sitting on a binder on page 62.

> My parishioners must clearly understand that they cannot arrange with anyone, mason or otherwise, to erect a memorial in the Church-yard without first having obtained my permission to do so, and my approval of the design and inscription. The Church-yard is *my* freehold, and parishioners have no more right to put up anything in it without my sanction, than I have to erect a stone, or a fort, or anything else in their grounds without permission.

There was certainly no cosy squire-parson relationship during his incumbency. This parson objected strongly to the Squire shooting over his glebe. The Coryton Game Book was produced which showed the exact number of game birds that the parson had accepted — and presumably eaten.

Yet, in spite of his firm stand on matters of principle, the relations between church and chapel at this time remained, if not cordial, at least charitable. There was a little rivalry, and many jokes told against one another. The story was told of the Rector's wife in an adjoining parish who met the sexton, dressed in his best clothes, hurrying toward the chapel. "Why, John", she cried, horrified, "Surely you are not going to the Meeting-house? I should have thought that you would be the very last man in the parish to go to that place." "So I be Ma'am," replied the Sexton, "all the rest have gone on a long time since." Then there were those in the Church who felt like R S Hawker of Morwenstow, who had written:

> O for the poor man's church again
>   With one roof over all;
> Where the true hearts of Cornishmen
>   Might beat beside the wall;
> The altars where in holier days
>   Our fathers were forgiven,
> Who went, with meek and faithful ways,
>   Through the old aisles to heaven.

But, whatever the differences, there was no hostility. During these first years of the twentieth century, when both the parish church and the two chapels were well-attended, the spiritual life of the people of Quethiock was catered for as it had not been since the Middle Ages. The Church services were held in a building once again enriched and made beautiful by the skill of William Willimott, the services enhanced by noble music from a fine organ. The second edition of *Hymns Ancient and Modern*, with a supplement, had been published in 1889 with the best of Charles Wesley's hymns, and many of the excellent hymns composed during the nineteenth century. There were also many translations of very early hymns, for example those by Bernard of Clairvaux, (1091-1153) such as, "Jesu, the very thought of Thee", and "O Jesus, King most wonderful", as well as others by St Francis of Assisi, Thomas Aquinas, and many others from the early centuries of the Christian era.

Augustus Wix wore himself out in the service of his church and parish, and died prematurely, leaving a widow and two little daughters of five and seven. *The Cornish Times*, in an obituary notice, said of him:

> The Rev. J A Wix had a very pronounced personality and held very definite views on matters concerning the Church. As a parish priest he kept himself thoroughly in touch with his people and visited among them with untiring zeal. He put the bells in order (1902) and obtained a fine organ for the Church (1903-5). September, 1905, when the organ was 'opened' was a personal triumph for the Vicar.
>
> He was a man of wide culture and many gifts, a nature lover and a keen photographer. He helped with comic songs at village concerts played cricket with his parish team and was a deadly lob bowler. He was a versatile man who was nevertheless an earnest, hard-working priest.

The obiturary ended by quoting the last verse of a hymn composed by Rev. J A Wix.

> Renew my will from day to day,
> Blend it with Thine, and take away
> All that now makes it hard to say,
>   "Thy will be done".

    He was buried in the churchyard that he guarded so zealously, and which is now full, within its circle of walls, the last burial being that of Ann Cannon, born a Snell, in March 1949, aged 92. It is a quiet place of mossy paths, and grey tombstones spotted with silver and yellow lichens, leaning with age under the weeping willows. Here lie the lucky people, the last to live here as part of a close-knit agricultural community which still preserved joy in daily work and pride in craftsmanship. These men and women had a real sense of personal achievement and satisfaction because, in their day, thrift and hard work were rewarded, and the work of food production was of primary importance. They enjoyed good health because they took a great deal of exercise and ate good, fresh food. They were happy because they were solvent, largely self-sufficient, and secure. They had no need to fear unemployment, nor inflation, let alone a total collapse of the nation's economy. The terms under which they farmed were dictated by the needs of good husbandry, their rents were modest, and the Corytons gave them a great deal in return. Their farming methods were not imposed upon them by faceless politicians juggling madly between cheap food and dear oil. Here they lie, these long rows of Cannons and Roseveares, these clusters of Higmans and Harrises, these many, many Snells scattered about, the Pollards, the Wenmoths, and all the others. Here too, a good parish priest to the end, lies Augustus Wix among his flock, quiet now, like all the rest. The sundial of the south wall of the church reminds us, "So soon passeth it away", but there is really no need for a reminder, not here.

    Standly proudly by the lower churchyard wall, the tall Celtic cross has a different message, of a spiritual permanence beyond this visible human impermanence. Here, in and around this holy place, lie many bones, the pagan ones first and deepest. Hereabouts lived the strong tribe of Iron Age Celts who fortified Cadson Bury and raised a small earthwork at nearby Hammett. These pagans, who are not to be confused with our modern city pagans, were neither irreligious, nor were they nihilists. They sensed the great mystery in the commonplace and reverenced sun and water. Here in this south-facing meadow was sun, and here too was water. Moreover when the first Christian missionaries came to Cornwall they chose places already sacred to the local tribe in which to celebrate Mass and preach the Gospel. Then, after Cadoc and his fellow missionaries had converted the pagans and the great granite Cross had been fashioned and raised up, many Celtic Christians must have been buried here. Next came the Saxon Christians, for with the founding of a Saxon Cornish bishopric at St German's, and of the great Saxon Abbey at Tavistock, the Saxon Christian church here must have flourished. Then came the conquering Normans who confiscated the Abbey's rich manor of Trebeigh in St Ive and much else beside. Domesday records three manors for Quethiock, Hammett, Leigh and Penpoll. Down came the Saxon church and up went a Norman one, so now the bones are those of Norman Christians owing allegiance to the Pope. After the Reformation the parishioners buried here became Anglican Christians, some of them reluctantly if the Great Western Rebellion is to be believed, and finally, there are Methodist Christians. All these good people, so far apart in time, in human experience, and in manner of worship, lie together in this holy place at peace. Quethiock's tall Celtic Cross stands as a benediction to them all, a magnificent symbol of Christian unity.

Miss Eileen Riddle, born in 1895, has lived in the parish of Quethiock all her life and is one of the few still living there who can remember it before 1919. She has kept in touch with old friends and her address book became very important as a means of contacting them. St. Hugh's means a great deal to her and she has happy memories of singing in Truro Cathedral's Choir Festivals. With her welcoming smile, her excellent memory and keen sense of humour, my visits have been a pleasure as well as a source of information.

Mr William Jane in the cosy parlour of the Blunts cottage in which he was born and still lives, with 'Morning Glory', his beautiful Blue Persian, alas known simply as 'Pussy'. Mr Jane's mother was born in 1862, a daughter of Henry Bennett the blacksmith. She married James Jane in 1883 and it was in this cottage that she reared her nine children. Mr Jane, a batchelor, is a staunch Methodist and is also seen on page 98.

Mr and Mrs Wallace Welch in their Quethiock garden. Mr Welch recently retired, has been a farm worker all his life, as his father was before him. Born the eldest of six children he had to begin to work as soon as possible to augment the family income. He worked for Mr John Tamblyn, at Holwood, for many years and is the very last farm worker to live in the village. He has been an active member of the Parish Council for over thirty years and a School Manager of his old school for twelve. Mrs Welch's mother was a Higman and her grandfather is holding a sheaf of wheat in the photograph at Trehunsey on page 62.

111

## ACKNOWLEDGEMENTS

*Treasured family photographs were lent willingly by many people chief among them being: Major Jeffery Coryton. Mrs Lodder and Mrs Willis (daughters of the Rev. J.A. Wix), Mr R. Wills, Mr & Mrs R. Cannon, Mr L. Wenmoth, Miss E Riddle, Mr and Mrs F. Bate, Mr and Mrs N. Hocking, Mrs P Bartlett, Mr W. Jane, Mrs C. Snell, Miss G. Mutton and Mr D. Davey.*

*Mr Tom Harris, of 'Ferndale' studios, took many of the old village photographs and the Rev. Wix many others. All of these, and more, have been carefully copied by Mr John Rapson, of Liskeard, who, luckily for me, is not only an excellent professional photographer but also a Cornish Bard, "Covather Derevyans, Recorder of Buildings", and has therefore brought keen interest as well as expertise to this record. Specially for this book he has photographed the exterior and interior of Blunts Methodist Church, the interior of Blunts Mission Church and the exterior of Quethiock Methodist Church; also the portraits of Miss Riddle, Mr Jane (both at home with 'Morning Glory' and also showing the harvest rick) and Mr and Mrs Welch.*

*The engraving of old Pentillie Castle, which is in the famous local collection of Mr Eric Putman, owner of The Cornish Times, is photographed by his kind permission. The busy staff of that paper have always helped cheerfully when I wanted to consult back files at inconvenient times.*

*Finally my grateful thanks to my husband, James Snell Wenmoth, not only because he was born in Quethiock, and so made me, by marriage, a member of one of its old farm families, but also because he has willingly helped me gather information and has endured with fortitude my sketchy housekeeping while writing it all down.*

© 1977 MARY FRENCH

ISBN 0 9502825 6 1

PUBLISHED by GLASNEY PRESS, Falmouth.

Designed and Produced by Oxford Print Consultants,
8 The Roundway, Headington, Oxford.